CALLING

Gospel Truths
to Guide Your Quest for
PASSIONATE, PURPOSEFUL WORK

Jeff Thompson, PhD
Stuart Bunderson, PhD

BYU Academic
Publishing

Copyright © 2013 Jeffery Thompson and Stuart Bunderson

Revised edition ©2015 Jeffery Thompson and Stuart Bunderson

ALL RIGHTS RESERVED.

No part of this work covered by the copyright herein may be reproduced or used in any form or by any means—graphic, electronic, or mechanical, including photocopying, recording, taping, web distribution or information storage and retrieval systems—without the written permission of the publisher.

ISBN: 9781611650150

For more information or permission to use material from this text or product contact:

BYU Academic Publishing

3991 WSC

Provo, UT 84602

Tel (801) 422—6231

Fax (801) 422—0070

academicpublishing@byu.edu

To report ideas or text corrections email us at:

textideas@byu.edu

1st Printing

Contents

CHAPTER 1
What Should I Do With My Life? 1

CHAPTER 2
What Does It Mean to Have a Calling? 9

CHAPTER 3
Who Gets a Calling? 31

CHAPTER 4
Spiritual Gifts and Callings. 49

CHAPTER 5
The Calling that Chooses You 69

CHAPTER 6
Families and Callings. 99

CHAPTER 7
Isn't a Calling Supposed to Be Fun?. 119

CHAPTER 8
Callings and Fame 137

CHAPTER 9
It's Not All About Work 157

CHAPTER 10

>   Mapping Out Your Life's Work: An Exercise 179

APPENDIX 1

>   Examples of Step 2 203

APPENDIX 2

>   Examples of Step 4 207

>   Acknowledgments 211

CHAPTER 1

What Should I Do With My Life?

What do you want to be when you grow up?

It's a question that small children love and adults fear. When you were a kid, your answer to that question may have changed from day to day. But it didn't bother you in the least to be inconsistent. At that age, the future was an exciting playground of possibilities.

But something probably happened to you along the way. Maybe an adult laughed at your wish to be an astronaut. Or someone chided your lack of ambition when you said you wanted to be a mom. Perhaps you found out that you weren't quite as gifted at some things as you thought you were. You didn't get the summer job you really wanted. You met people who were miserable in their careers. You couldn't find a major that excited you. You realized that running a household involves a lot of drudgery. You had a mean boss that made work a torture. You found out that people in your field get little money or respect. People you love disapproved of your goals. You felt underappreciated. You struggled to pay the mortgage. You got laid off.

When you come face to face with the disappointing gap between your childhood ideals and the jarring realities of adult life, it's easy to lose that innocent sense of excitement about the possibilities for your life. Instead of viewing your life's work as an opportunity for growth and expression, you start to see it as a burden, a source of self-doubt and anxiety. You feel a bit like Adam and Eve, driven out of your state of naïve innocence into a work world filled with thistles and thorns and the prospect of earning your bread in sweat and sorrow (Genesis 3: 17–18). You may even conclude that drudgery is just meant to be.

This book invites you to pause before you close the door on childlike wonder about your mission in life. Children don't typically say things like, "Nah, I don't want a career. I just want to get to retirement as quickly as I can." Instead, they are almost universally eager to enter a world of doing things that matter and that help them grow. They want to contribute. They want to discover, to help, to express. Granted, their expectations are somewhat distorted (which is just as well, to protect their idealism). But their motives are pure and genuine. They have an innate conviction that they have something important to offer the world.

We are really talking about *you* here, because you were that child. At some point, you felt that you could simply choose what you wanted to be. Your parents may have taught you that you are a child of God, with divine qualities and unlimited potential. So why *shouldn't* you expect to do great things? Even if you weren't taught as a child that you are the offspring of a Heavenly Father, you probably felt—at least somewhere along the way—a sense of implicit worth, a bone-deep affirmation that there was a spark of divinity within you, that you had something unique to offer to the world.

We submit that this was not just childhood naivety. The feeling that you can *contribute* is a gift from Heavenly Father. He knows your potential and wants you to magnify your talents. We invite you to heed the childlike voice within that assures you of your divine worth. Like any spiritual impression, it is there to "guide you into all truth" (John 16:13), including divine answers to the question "What should I do with my life?"

From Idealism to Anxiety

As university professors, we talk to hundreds of students about their career plans. What we hear is a lot of anxiety. Students lose sleep over which class they should sign up for, let alone daunting questions like "What should my career be?" or "What is my life's purpose?" In fact, many of our students seem absolutely paralyzed by such questions—fearing that if they get the answer wrong, they are doomed to a life of dissatisfaction or, worse, that they will somehow miss the path that God has charted for them.

It isn't just college students who are consumed by doubt and anxiety about professional choices. We also teach seasoned professionals who question their path. They are pained by the irony that they are still wondering—in their 40s, 50s, or beyond—what they want to be when they "grow up." Sometimes they feel like failures because their path hasn't taken a clear, defined shape. We also sometimes teach stay-at-home moms hoping to reenter the work force. They worry that they have missed the opportunity to develop talents and make a living. We have learned from them that many women who choose the noble path of family caregiver nevertheless continue to struggle with questions about whether they are fully realizing their purpose in life.

It can be heart-wrenching to watch people struggle with these questions. The anxiety consumes them. They long for that feeling of excitement and certainty that they had as a child, but instead face nagging questions about whether they are even doing the right thing. It's no wonder that we sometimes view our work as a distraction from, or even destructive to, the happiness that comes from the best things in life, like family and service in the Lord's kingdom.

Can it really be Heavenly Father's plan for you to feel anxiety, fear, or resignation about your working life, especially if you spend the majority of your waking hours there? Shouldn't the gospel of Jesus Christ give you a path toward clarity and peace about the work you do?

We know that "God hath not given us the spirit of fear; but of power, and of love, and of a sound mind" (2 Timothy 1:7). Anxiety is clearly *not* one of the "fruits of the spirit" (see Galatians 5:22–23). So it doesn't seem likely that professional fear and anguish are consistent with Heavenly Father's desires for you.

At the same time, the Lord makes no promise that work will come easy to you, or that the right professional path will always be crystal clear. Making important decisions almost always requires intensely diligent intellectual effort as you "study it out in your mind" (D&C 9:7). And occasionally feeling lost might just be part of God's plan for your growth. Even God's chosen people, the ancient Israelites, spent 40 years wandering in a wilderness before they found their promised land. We mortals aren't meant to have easy answers and a carefree stroll through our lives. Given what we know about how God tutors his children, perhaps we should be a little grateful that our quest for purpose is a poorly marked path, and often rocky.

Developing that kind of gratitude is easier said than done, of course, which is why we have decided to write this book. It is a book for people who are trying to find their calling in life, who want to contribute more to the world. We wrote it especially for people who feel some uncertainty—maybe even anxiety—about where they are, or the path ahead. But it's also an invitation to think about the spiritual roots of the work you do (whether in the office or at home or elsewhere), and to strive for greater meaning and purpose during the many hours that you spend in your working life.

We invite you to take this book personally. You'll find that it includes many stories—both heroic and ordinary—of people who are striving to find meaning in their daily lives and work. The book is, in part, a result of years of academic research, both our own and that of our scholarly colleagues. It's also a result of frank conversations with countless people who we have taught and been taught by. And, most fundamentally, it's a product of our study of scriptural teachings and gospel principles as they relate to work and its place in a disciple's life. We have found that the restored gospel of Jesus Christ has a great deal to teach about finding your calling in life. In fact, just as we believe that the greatest wellsprings of family happiness flow to those who center their lives on the Savior's teaching, we testify that the greatest professional fulfillment is only available when you build your career on Jesus Christ's gospel, which allows you to keep your profession in its proper perspective.

Why We Sometimes Feel Lost

Because we intend this book to be personal, we'll start by getting personal ourselves. Both of us are academic experts on meaningful work, so you might think that we figured out our paths in life pretty easily. Not true! Although we both absolutely love what we do and feel like we have found our calling in life, we were both educated not just academically, but also in the school of hard knocks. Both of us have struggled at different stages of our lives to find peace in the direction we were heading. We experienced surprising setbacks and roadblocks that confused us, and sometimes even gave us a feeling of crisis.

For Jeff, these experiences came early in his career. At times, he felt utterly adrift, as if he had somehow missed the right path and could never get back on it. For Stuart, the anxiety and angst came later, as he questioned what type of legacy he wanted to leave through his teaching and research, and how he wanted to spend the latter half of his career. These questions caused many sleepless nights for both of us.

As disorienting as those personal crises were, we don't regret having them. In hindsight, those moments are essential parts of the tapestry of our lives and careers. Each thread that felt out of place at the time has come to provide structure to the pattern of our lives. Those threads helped us to refine our sense of calling. They are now proof to us that all things "work together for good to them that love God, to them who are the *called* according to his purpose" (Romans 8:28, emphasis added). Our tapestries are not yet finished; we still get snarled up with confusion now and then. But because we can see God's hand in our past, we feel confident that He will continue to guide us in the future.

What You Can Expect

We have organized this book around seven major themes, each of which challenges a false doctrine of work that the world promotes. You might think of them as seven cardinal heresies about work and careers. In Chapter 2, we show where these heresies came from and describe what a "calling in life" means from a gospel perspective. In Chapters 3 through 9, we tackle each heresy and show how to dispel it. Each of those chapters ends with a brief section called "What Can I Do Now?" These sections are meant to be acted upon, not just read. We will ask you to consider some tough personal questions, to reflect and write about your responses, and sometimes even to step out of your comfort zone to try out an activity or engage with people around you. We have designed these activities so that they are applicable to almost anyone, regardless of life stage or profession. And when we use the words "career" and "profession," we are including the vital work of homemaking as well.

Finally, Chapter 10 walks you through an exercise that we strongly encourage you to complete. It builds upon the questions in the previous chapters and helps you draw a diagram (we call it a "calling map") to help you think more carefully about your own calling and how you will find it.

Despite its "workbook" feel, we don't claim that this book is a step-by-step manual for discovering your calling. There is no precise formula for finding your life's mission. It can only be done by "studying it out in your mind," seeking spiritual insight, and engaging in trial and error to learn about yourself. So don't expect to have a nicely packaged "answer" when you reach the last page. If you do what we ask, however, we can promise a deepened insight into your gifts and unique potential, a greater sense of hope that the Lord will be able to use you professionally to bless His children, and an ability to exercise more courage in making personal and professional choices in the pursuit of your calling.

Every journey goes more smoothly when there is a skilled navigator along for the ride. As children of a Heavenly Father, we have access to a perfect and omniscient navigator. Despite our years of academic study about callings and meaningful work, we recognize that our knowledge is vastly incomplete when compared to the knowledge that the Holy Ghost can convey to you personally about your own specific journey. You may find that some of the things we present do not align perfectly with the inspiration you have received about your Heavenly Father's plan for you. And although we rely heavily upon scriptures to teach the principles we want to share, we claim no ecclesiastical authority for them, nor do we speak on behalf of the Lord or His Church. Instead, we simply invite you to ponder and reflect on the things we have learned and to seek the Spirit's guidance in their proper application in your life.

A Note From the Authors

One challenge of co-authoring a book with a personal tone is how to share personal stories. We both draw heavily on our life experiences in this book. We will frequently refer to ourselves in the third person ("Jeff" or "Stuart") so that it is clear which of us had the experience we are sharing.

Notes

CHAPTER 2

What Does It Mean to Have a Calling?

Jeff shares the following experience:

I had a wonderful boss when I worked at the headquarters of a large shoe company that specializes in inexpensive footwear. He was a consummate corporate climber, completely energized by the rough-and-tumble of office politics. I was pretty sure that he lived for the thrill of doing business. (I, on the other hand, most certainly did not.) He was never very sentimental about work and didn't seem to give much thought to any higher purpose.

One day, out of the blue, he surprised me by saying pensively, "You know, Jeff, I've finally figured it out. We sell self-esteem."

"Excuse me... how's that?"

"We sell self-esteem!," he reiterated. "We put affordable shoes on the feet of kids who don't have much money so that they can feel good about themselves at school. We sell self-esteem!"

My first reaction (which I kept to myself) was "That's preposterous. Kids who wear our shoes get mocked at school. Our shoes aren't cool enough."

My second reaction was, "Wow, even my boss, who thrives on corporate adrenaline, is in desperate need of deeper meaning in his work."

Through our research, we have come to believe that the desire for meaningfulness is almost universal. Human beings seem to be wired for a sense of purpose.

This is not to say, however, that people won't put forth great effort for material rewards. They do. But we think that the great theologian Harry Emerson Fosdick put it best:

Men will work hard for money; they will work harder for other men. But men will work hardest of all when they are dedicated to a cause.[1]

It turns out that Fosdick was exactly right. Yale University's Amy Wrzesniewski and her colleagues have shown that people do tend to fall into one of these three categories. Some people work just to make a living. Scholars call that a "job orientation." Others work because it gives them an opportunity to move up in the world and build a reputation. That is called a "career orientation." Still others work because of a deep sense of purpose—a desire to serve a cause they are passionate about. We refer to that as a "calling orientation."

Fosdick hit the nail on the head in his prediction as well: research shows that people with a calling orientation do in fact exhibit remarkably high motivation. They sacrifice more for their work, and gain more satisfaction from it as well. But does this mean that everyone *should* have a calling orientation? Is there anything wrong with just having a job and working to get by? What should work to mean to you, after all?

Perhaps you might reason that your spiritual life provides all the meaning you need. After all, the gospel bestows a deep sense of purpose in families and in faith. Should you just do your worldly chores dutifully and quickly so that you can set them aside and get to the really important things? Perhaps if you put too much stake in the earthly purposes of your work, you will be distracted from pursuing eternal purposes in other parts of your life.

The problem with this reasoning is that it draws a hard line between your work life and your spiritual life. And the Lord has taught that "all things unto me are spiritual" (D&C 29:34). So it would be a mistake to ignore how Heavenly Father views your work, and to fail to consider how it impacts your spirit. In fact, the doctrines of the restored gospel have many things to say about work, some of which are unique in all the religious world. To appreciate what is unique about the restored gospel's depiction of work, let's take a brief dive into history to see how mankind's view of work has changed over time.

Work: A Curse or a Calling?

Anciently, work didn't have a very good reputation. Digging back into early recorded history, it's clear that people saw work as demeaning and as a threat to their happiness. Take the ancient Greeks, for instance. Here was a society that flourished artistically and philosophically, at least for a period of time. But the grandeur of Ancient Greece was built on the backs of slaves.

How could such an enlightened society condone enslaving fellow human beings? Because the Greeks saw work as a galling distraction from the sublime pursuits of the mind. How could you appreciate philosophy, engage in civic debate, or enjoy artistic and architectural achievements if you also had to sweep the floors, maintain the roads, and prepare the food? Living the good life meant escaping the burdens of menial labor. Slavery was the convenient, if unsavory, answer.

The Greeks were not the only society that equated labor with servitude. Even after abolishing slavery, most Western cultures maintained clear distinctions between the working class and the privileged. For instance, having a profession—even a lucrative one—was a sign of social inferiority during the Regency Period in England, as memorably depicted by Jane Austen and the Bronte sisters. People of the highest quality did not work. They depended on servants and serfs to support their privileged lifestyles. For much of the history of humankind, people have not viewed labor (whether vocational or domestic) as meaningful, but instead as something you have to avoid in order to lead a happy and graceful life.

Religious views of work over the ages have not been much more enthusiastic. Consider how the ancient Hebrew and Christian traditions interpreted the Fall of Adam. The Old Testament records that God placed Adam and Eve in a plentiful garden paradise and gave them dominion over the earth. Adam and Eve didn't need to lift a finger to earn a living. Only when they committed what religious traditions consider to be the "original sin"—partaking the forbidden fruit—did Adam and Eve have to start worrying about labor. God tells Adam, "In the sweat of thy face shalt thou eat thy bread," which may seem like a severe penalty considering how easy it had been to find a meal beforehand.

For early religious traditions, work was literally a curse. God's children would only escape that curse when they "return unto the ground" (Genesis 3:19) at death, and once again became part of the dust from which they were formed. If you follow that line of reasoning, you can see that heaven must be a place completely devoid of work. To early religionists, man's greatest potential was to return to a paradisiacal state without any labor.

Similar to the Greeks, early Christian sects believed that work was an impediment to the best things in life—specifically, closeness to God. How could you come closer to God, they reasoned, if you were distracted by agricultural labor or time-consuming craftsmanship? Monastic orders and asceticism emerged as ways for believers to escape the worldly demands of labor and devote themselves to God. The lifestyle of the monk, the nun, and the ascetic depended on the labor of others who donated (willingly or otherwise) the sweat of their brow so that the favored few could pursue spiritual enlightenment, free from the burdens of labor. Students of the Book of Mormon might recognize in this teaching shades of the doctrine of the false prophet Nehor, who argued that "every priest and teacher... ought not to labor with their hands, but that they ought to be supported by the people" (Alma 1:3).

In summary, for most of the history of the world, the idea that work could be meaningful and satisfying was a completely alien concept. The only option for most people was to eke out a living doing whatever their fathers and their fathers' fathers had done, just to keep bread on the table.

All of that changed with Martin Luther, who revolutionized how the world looks at work. Luther saw the fallacy in viewing work as a curse that could be pawned off on others. He taught that work is a divinely appointed privilege that allows you to participate in God's providence toward his children. As long as your work serves mankind, it allows you to partner with God in blessing His children. So, to Luther, work isn't a distraction from God, but a way to become more like Him!

Luther was the one who introduced to the world the idea of a professional "calling" in life. He argued that, because God uses our professional efforts to bless His children, we have a sacred duty to work diligently at them, and to do so with our hearts fixed on service. As he stated, "A Christian tailor... will say: I make these clothes because God has bidden me to do so, so that I can earn a living, so that I can help and serve my neighbor."[2] This was a radical departure from the view that work was a necessary evil brought about by Adam's sin. Suddenly, the Christian world began to see work as a divine summons—an invitation from God to sustain ourselves materially even as we bless others around us. Work and faith went hand-in-hand. As Lee Hardy, a scholar of Luther's teachings, noted: "As we pray each morning for our daily bread, people are already busy at work in the bakeries."[3]

Another great Reformer, John Calvin, fleshed out Luther's ideas by teaching people *how* to find their callings. While Luther believed your calling was simply to do the profession you were born into, Calvin argued that your calling originates in the unique and particular talents that God has given you. He taught that you have an obligation to discover those gifts and to seek out ways to use them in the service of your fellowmen. As he put it, "For as God bestows any ability or gift upon any of us, he binds us to such as have need of us and as we are able to help."[4]

Notice the language that Calvin uses here. He's not suggesting that having a talent is a nice little blessing that could come in handy. He is preaching that talents *bind* us. They *obligate* us to serve. For both Luther and Calvin, a calling isn't a matter of going out into the world to find your personal bliss and make as much money as you can along the way. A calling is a summons from God. Of course, it brings blessings upon the heads of those who answer it. But it is also a burden that demands sacrifice and the "sweat of thy brow." To the Reformers, work is inherently noble, and elevates people to a more God-like state.

It should be clear by now that the idea of a "calling in life" is of distinctly religious origin. After all, how could there be a calling without a "Caller?" Ironically, however, the modern world has clung doggedly to the idea of a calling while almost entirely abandoning its spiritual roots. Think about how people use the phrase "calling in life" today, and how universal it has become. You can walk into any corporate office and say, "you know, I've been thinking about what my calling in life is," and you won't get any funny looks. People will nod and understand that you are seeking to do something meaningful that is suited to your talents. But if you say, "You know, I've been trying to figure out what God wants me to do with my career," you might encounter awkward silence or an invitation to leave your religion at the door.

For most people today, calling is a completely secular concept. In fact, when we have interviewed people for our research about professional callings, God almost never comes up. Famed sociologist Max

Weber described it as follows: "The idea of duty in one's calling prowls about in our lives like the ghost of dead religious beliefs."[5] Surely Luther and Calvin are rolling over in their graves to see the way we have stripped work of its spiritual significance. They would surely frown on the way we have co-opted their sacred concept of calling to make it a secular buzzword. Are the religious beliefs that underlie calling really dead?

A Latter-day Saint Perspective

The scriptures of the restoration supply a strikingly different interpretation of the Fall of Adam than many Christian religions embrace. While the "orthodox" view is that Adam and Eve brought a tragic curse upon themselves because of their thoughtless disobedience, modern prophets have revealed that the transgression of Adam and Eve was essential for our growth and happiness. Far from being a tragedy, the Fall allowed Adam to say "because of my transgression my eyes are opened, and in this life I shall have joy, and again in the flesh I shall see God" (Moses 5:10). Eve added that the Fall provided us the blessing of having seed, of discerning good from evil, and knowing "the joy of our redemption and the eternal life which God giveth unto all the obedient" (Moses 5:11).

Adam and Eve are not speaking here like people who have been cursed. In fact, a careful reading of Moses Chapter 4 reveals that God *never did* curse Adam and Eve. The only curses spoken of are a curse upon the serpent in verse 20, and a curse upon the ground in verse 23. True, the curse upon the ground has a direct impact on Adam, because he has to till that ground to survive. The ground is cursed *for his sake*, after all. But this doesn't imply that Adam's work is accursed or demeaning—only that it will challenge and stretch him. The curse on the ground served to sanctify Adam, not enslave him to a brute existence.

There is even stronger evidence, though, that God doesn't consider work a curse. If you carefully read the scriptural account of Adam and Eve's experience in Eden, it becomes clear that the Lord gave them work even *before* the Fall occurred. Moses 3:15 teaches that the Lord put Adam "into the Garden of Eden, to dress it, and to keep it" before he ever partook of the forbidden fruit. (And this doesn't even count the work Adam put into naming all of the animals!). Clearly, there is little doctrinal basis for claiming that work itself is a fallen state of affairs. What changed after the Fall was simply the introduction of adversity into human work—the "thorns and thistles" that complicate our efforts.

Another thing that changed about work after the Fall is truly momentous. Using secular language, we might call it the introduction of incentives. Listen to what the Lord says immediately after the Fall: "By the sweat of thy face shalt thou eat bread" (Moses 4:25). Prior to that declaration, Adam and Eve didn't have to work for a reward. The Father provided for all their needs. Afterwards, their survival was contingent upon work. They had to think about maximizing the yield of their crops, and finding ways to get the most result from their limited supply of energy and resources. Whether Adam enjoyed his agricultural labors or not was beside the point. He was working for a reward.

This turn of events suggests that material incentives are a telestial phenomenon. They can curse your work because they destroy the purity of intent that accompanies your service to others. They propel you to think about selfish interests and may cause you to resent work that you otherwise might enjoy doing. As the title of one classic psychology book expresses it, the Fall of Adam has left us "Punished by Rewards."[6] Work isn't the curse. Self-absorption in the pursuit of rewards is.

Many other prophets, ancient and modern, reinforce the Protestant Reformers' doctrine that work is noble and godly. If you study the word "work" in scripture, you quickly find that God Himself labors. Consider how he describes what he does. Bringing about our immortality and eternal life is "my work and my glory" (Moses 1:39). He frequently refers to his efforts to restore the blessings of salvation as a "great and marvelous work."

The Book of Mormon provides examples of wise and great leaders who toiled with their hands. Prophets worked. As Alma reports: "I have labored even from the commencement of the reign of the judges until now, with mine own hands for my support" (Alma 30: 32). Military leaders worked. Captain Moroni was "a man who did labor exceedingly for the welfare and safety of his people" (Alma 48:12). And even kings were not above getting their hands dirty. King Benjamin said "even I, myself, have labored with mine own hands that I might serve you, and that ye should not be laden with taxes" (Mosiah 2:14).

Virtually every description of labor in the scriptures of the restoration depicts work as a blessing. Not only do the Book of Mormon people experience prosperity when they work hard, they also experience peace. The connection between industriousness and peace occurs over and over again (see Mosiah 10:4-5; Mosiah 23:5; Alma 23:18; Helaman 6:13; Ether 10:22-28). Captain Moroni demonstrates one reason for this relationship. He made sure that his prisoners of war were put to work building fortress walls "because it was easy to guard them while at their labor" (Alma 53:5). Engaging in worthwhile work focuses our minds and soothes our unruly spirits.

Even in the temple, a place of profound peace and repose, we see temple *workers* reverently but busily engaged in their sacred labors. Sitting in the waiting room after an endowment session one day, Stuart was struck by the quiet busy-ness of the happy temple workers—all volunteers laboring without financial reward of any kind. It struck him that the energetic vitality of a busy temple is probably an accurate picture of what our post-mortal labors will look like. Surely we won't be lounging about after we pass from mortality, since the saints who die "shall rest from all their labors *here*, and shall continue their works" (D&C 124:86, emphasis added; see also D&C 138:57). Work can't possibly be a mortal curse if the saints will continue to labor after they have entered paradise.

The restored gospel reintroduces the missing spiritual core of work. It reinforces the radical Reformation idea that work is a partnership with God. Modern scripture teaches that working in mortality is how you prepare and perfect your ability to work in the eternities to do the things that God does.

So What Exactly Is a Calling?

Now that we have explored the history of work and the way LDS doctrine portrays it, you might be wondering what a "calling" really is. Of course, the word is very common in the Mormon vernacular: Every active adult member should expect a calling at church. Your church calling may be well-suited to your talents, or perhaps a chance to develop new ones. Church callings come through inspiration from priesthood authority, and last only until the Spirit directs a leader to extend a release. Church callings are thus variable, developmental, and temporary. They don't really capture what Luther and Calvin meant by a calling in life. For the purposes of this book, we need to develop a clear picture of what a calling in life is—and what it is not.

Let's start with the contemporary definition. Today's secular version of calling goes something like this: "When I find my calling in life, it will mean that I am doing work that I love to do. Work will feel like play, and my job will consistently energize me. It will be something I'm good at, and something that people recognize me for." This sounds pretty appealing, doesn't it! Anyone would like to be able to do work that is both fun and fulfilling. The contemporary view of calling boils down to a dream job.

It's also a little bit dangerous.

The more you hear about how callings bring people unfettered professional bliss, the more you might feel cheated (or like a failure) if your work is difficult, painful, or goes unrecognized. The contemporary version reverberates through the mantra of the Millennial Generation: You can change the world, and you can be deeply satisfied doing it. Although there are wonderful things about that mantra, what you don't hear from this contemporary version of calling is that even meaningful work *is still work*, that it is sometimes agonizing and frustrating, and that many people have to struggle at seemingly insignificant tasks for years before they master the skills that allow them to make a real difference in the world. This modern notion of calling, with its focus on self-gratification, is actually eroding away the path that leads people to lasting meaningfulness. We fear that today's youth will ultimately find that the promise of an easy and blissful calling was hollow. They may become jaded long before they have had the impact that is within their capacity.

As a result of these concerns, our research has investigated whether the classical spiritual view of calling is really dead. Might the Protestant Reformers' scripturally inspired view of calling still be accessible in your career and family endeavors? Can you revive the "ghost" of these "dead religious beliefs" so that you think more realistically about your calling, and find meaning in your work that will stand the test of time and adversity?

A Trip to the Zoo

We decided to begin our scholarly exploration in an unlikely place—the zoo. Why would we study zookeepers to learn about calling? Most importantly, we chose zookeepers because we wanted to learn from people who were passionate about their work, but who aren't in it for money or for fame and recognition.

It turns out that zookeepers fit these criteria beautifully. The average zookeeper at the time of our study made less than $25,000 per year—nearly poverty wages in the US. The majority of those we studied had to have other sources of income (a second job or financial support from family, for instance) in order to make ends meet.

And you don't get famous in zookeeping. Zookeepers have few opportunities for promotion beyond front-line supervisor, so they aren't gaining status by climbing the corporate ladder. The work of a zookeeper can be dirty, smelly, and dangerous, so the public tends to view zoo work as menial and distasteful. An elephant handler told us, for instance, that a nun came by with a group of young students while a fellow zookeeper was cleaning the elephant enclosure. As the nun gathered her charges to move on, she turned to the children and said (loudly enough to be within earshot of the elephant handler), "See the kind of job you get when you don't finish your education." Ironically, this zookeeper had a masters degree. Three-fourths of the zookeepers we surveyed had at least a bachelor's degree.

In short, zookeeping is dangerous and dirty (we'll leave the details to your imagination). It pays extraordinarily little. It gives you virtually no opportunity to get promoted or get a big raise. It comes with some social stigmas attached. Sounds miserable, right?

But zookeepers represent the happiest group of employees we have ever studied. Their sense of meaningfulness is off the charts. We surveyed more than 1300 zookeepers from around the country, in every major zoo. 84% of them agreed that they have a meaningful job that makes a difference. Only about 6% were thinking of leaving their work for another profession. And 88% of them agreed that their job represented their calling in life. But what really struck us was the way they talked about their work. One of the questions we asked them was "what would be grounds for divorce from the zoo?" We expected them to cite the common litany of complaints: being underappreciated, being underpaid, poor management, etc. But what we heard absolutely dumbfounded us. Here are some typical responses to that question:

"There's not much that they could do to get me to quit."

"I can't think what would cause me to leave."

"I don't think there's anything they could do that would make me leave."

Eventually, we started asking zookeepers if they would finally walk away if management made decisions that hurt the animals. Their answer: No. That would be even a *stronger* reason to stay, because someone needs to protect the animals.

We realized that we were dealing with something pretty special here. These were people who were willing to give up financial stability, physical comfort, and sometimes even personal safety in order to take care of captive animals. Even if management treated them poorly, they were going to stay put and protect their animals. As we reviewed pages and pages of our interview notes, we began to see an overwhelming common theme. Zookeepers' work is not a job or a career; it's a calling. Many of the zookeepers used that very word. Others called it their "niche" or "what I was born to do." No matter how they described it, there was clearly something unique about zookeepers. We started wondering what exactly this sense of calling was. Where did it come from? How did the zookeepers know they had it? And—perhaps most importantly—is it something that you can find in other professions as well? Is there the potential for you to feel like a zookeeper about your own work?

The Zookeeper's Calling

To answer those questions, we dove back into our field notes. And the answers almost leapt off the pages at us. Happily, the themes we found there have almost universal applicability—which means that you can develop a version of the zookeeper's calling for yourself. The themes also resonate beautifully with the teachings of the restored gospel. Discovering those themes was one of those rare experiences for us when academic findings vibrate with spiritual truth. We realized that the zookeepers weren't just teaching us how to be happy in the challenging world of caring for captive animals. They were teaching us enduring principles that can bless and enrich the work lives of anyone who is willing to take them seriously.

Of all the principles we learned from zookeepers, three struck us as virtually definitional. They are:

1. Your calling in life is rooted in your unique spiritual gifts.

Of course, zookeepers didn't use the phrase "spiritual gifts." But it was obvious that they recognized in themselves a unique talent, ability, or interest that made them different from other people. Most of them had discovered very early in life that they were "hardwired" to work with animals. Here is what some of them had to say:

"It's a part of who I am, and I don't know if I can explain that. When you use that expression 'it's in your blood,' like football coaches and players can never retire because it's in their blood. Whatever my genetic makeup is, I'm geared toward animals."

"I was always interested in animals ever since I was a kid. I drove my mom nuts catching bugs and worms and frogs and salamanders, bringing home anything I could find. Butterflies. Stuff like that."

"It's a calling for me just because my whole life I've just been interested in animals. So looking back I should have known at some time I would be working with animals."

Most zookeepers just seem to know, to their very core, that they are "animal people." Recognizing their gifts tells them the type of person they are. You may have spiritual gifts that are more difficult to discern or apply. But as we'll explore in Chapter 4, you most definitely have them.

2. Your calling in life gives you sacred obligations to serve.

Zookeepers didn't actually use the word "sacred," but they described a *very* strong sense of obligation toward their animals. And this is where their definition of calling really starts to diverge from what the world teaches. Let's try stepping inside the head of a future zookeeper for a moment to see how their reasoning might play out:

Let's imagine that a young girl says to herself, "I'm an animal person. I have special abilities to interact with animals and I can love and care for them in ways that other people can't." As a child, just playing with her pets was probably a sufficient expression of this spiritual gift. But as she read more about animals and associated with other people like her, she had another realization: "There are animals in need! There are species that are dying out because their habitats are threatened. What can I do to help them survive and thrive?"

So now this young girl has discovered a crying need that is located precisely where her spiritual gifts lie. The moment that she discovers her calling as a zookeeper might sound like this: "Wait a minute, if I'm hardwired to help animals, and there are animals in need, then it is *up to me* to be the one to help them! Who else but someone like me can meet this need? I have an *obligation* to help these captive animals because of who I am." And thus, a zookeeper calling is born.

We have made up this little monologue to show you that callings reside at the intersection of your spiritual gifts and someone else's need in the world. Hopefully you are seeing that a calling isn't just about fun and self-gratification. It's about discovering that someone requires the very gifts you've been given. Once you make that connection, you can't look back. You simply *have* to use your gifts to serve.

That compulsive need to serve showed up in a lot of our interviews. Here are some exemplary quotes:

> "The animals never chose to be here and it's our responsibility to come in and give them the care that they need and make sure that they're healthy and happy."

> "If I don't stay then who's going to be here to make sure that the animals are taken care of the way I want them to be taken care of? I'm here for that."

> "There's a quote that I read somewhere that says that we become responsible for that we have obtained. That's kind of how I look at it. We obtained these animals… I mean, they have no other choice… They're stuck here. So I have to do what's best for them."

3. Your calling in life is revealed to you rather than chosen.

One last component of calling that our zookeeper research revealed was something that seemed to puzzle even the zookeepers themselves. The reason may be that they didn't take a spiritual view of their careers when they should have. A person of faith, for instance, recognizes the hand of God operating in his or her life. Rather than coincidences, they see evidence of heavenly intervention on their behalf. Elder David A. Bednar has referred to these as "tender mercies,"[7] and Elder Gerald N. Lund calls them "divine signatures."[8]

None of our zookeepers, however, said that God had guided them to their profession. But most of them used almost mystical language to describe the events and circumstances that guided led them, as if inevitably, toward their calling. Rather than God, they talked about luck, fate, or destiny. For example:

"I've always read a lot about [animals] and it kind of led me here. It was magical in a way."

"I just fell into the right places. And I'll admit being where I am right now is 50% me pushing to go in a certain direction and 50% luck. I mean, that part-time job I got when I first came here, I had nothing to do with it."

"So things kind of worked out the way they should… I kind of fell into this. Things just worked out real well."

"I was here two days and I knew this was what I was meant to do. There's people that have volunteered here for years, and they don't get a job. And I worked here a month and a half [and got one]. So it's kind of like my calling, I think."

So, even without faith in a divine "Caller," people discern something supernatural (even if they think it's just luck) guiding them toward their calling in life. For most of these people, their calling didn't come in a flash of insight. Instead, it was a slow and steady accumulation of experiences that just kept moving them forward, ultimately taking them where they could use their gifts to serve others.

It's not just zookeepers that point to some unknown external guiding force. We hear similar accounts from other people we have interviewed about their callings in life, including the bear whisperer, the Starbucks barista, and the people-centered CEO that you will meet later in this book. They all felt remarkably fortunate because the right doors had just somehow opened for them. They recognized that they couldn't have made it where they were on their own. Although they might not have recognized it at the time, hindsight gave them an undeniable sense that, somehow, the right doors—even unexpected ones—had opened for them.

Of course, viewed from a lens of faith, it is much easier to account for this mystical intervention of fate. Heavenly Father isn't a passive observer of your life, but is actively engaged in your tutelage and training. He has told you that the purpose of your existence is "that [you] might have joy" (2 Nephi 2:25). So you shouldn't be surprised that He orchestrates opportunities to help you find joy in the work you do. It's a great testimony of His love for His children that so many people—including those who don't believe in God—gradually find their lives shaping up to allow the expression of their best gifts.

All in all, these three insights that we gained from studying zookeepers give us a pretty good working definition of a calling in life. To put it all together, *you find your calling when life leads you to where your spiritual gifts allow you—and obligate you—to serve others.*

This definition is quite different from the contemporary idea that a calling is a dream job. In fact, the zookeeper calling is much closer to what Martin Luther and John Calvin had in mind. It's not about self-gratification, but about using your best gifts in selfless service. Of course, the Savior taught this principle far more powerfully and poetically than the Reformers. He said, "He that findeth his life shall lose it: and he that loseth his life for my sake shall find it" (Matthew 10:39). You may not immediately think of these words as career advice. But research about callings verifies what the Savior taught: losing yourself in service is a more direct route to happiness -- even professional happiness—than is seeking personal gain.

Gifts, Causes, and Circumstances

We will return to our zookeeper friends in future chapters to provide more insights about *how* you can find your calling in life. But we want to conclude this chapter with the story of a man whose life circumstances led him to a calling that he never could have anticipated. It's an inspiring and surprising example of how Heavenly Father can intervene to create circumstances that connect your spiritual gifts to the needs of His children.

Dr. Dale Hull experienced a major life change—not to mention a career change—in 1999. He was a highly successful OB/GYN physician in Salt Lake, but a freak trampoline accident suddenly rendered him quadriplegic. Because of his medical training, Dale knew at the moment of the accident that his life would never be the same again. Not only would he be a different type of husband and father, he also would never deliver another baby.

Dale's recovery was an arduous, and ultimately miraculous process. After two and a half years of intensive therapy, Dale regained much of his sensory and motor function, and was even able to walk the Olympic Torch as it made its way to the 2002 Winter Olympics in Salt Lake City, where he handed off to former Utah Jazz star Karl Malone. Despite his surprising return to mobility, however, Dale still lacked the manual dexterity to return to his obstetrics practice—his dream job. The door seemed to have slammed on his calling in life.

Dale now had no clear professional path to follow. How he could be of use to anyone? How could he provide for his family? Despite these consuming questions, he started to notice a critical need. Other spinal cord injury victims, inspired by Dale's story, were coming out of the woodwork to ask for his advice. They wanted to learn about the radical therapies he had undergone.

Dale learned that resources for these patients were extremely scarce, and few of them had the opportunity to receive the type of treatment he had benefitted from. In short order, Dale began to transition from being a physician to becoming a nonprofit founder and executive director. His organization, Neuroworx, provides cutting-edge treatment and rehabilitation for spinal cord injury patients, who travel to his clinic from all over the western United States.

Dale could easily have shut himself away and resented the cruel hand of fate. He could have concluded that his calling was at an end. Instead, he found a way to combine his medical expertise with his unique and unexpected life experience. Life brought him a new calling—one that provides him a deep sense of passion and fulfillment. In fact, today Dale expresses *gratitude* for the tragedy that changed his life. He is thankful that the Lord led him to his new calling.

Dale's story drives home the principles of calling that the zookeepers teach us. It reminds us that a professional calling isn't just about what you love to do. It's also about *using* your unique talents and experiences—both the fortuitous and tragic ones—to serve in a way that only *you* can.

Heresies

Our research and our scripture study has helped us realize that there is a deep chasm between modern beliefs and enduring truths about work. We are convinced that people who are truly and deeply satisfied with their working lives are following the Lord's model of work, even if they don't recognize it.

On the other hand, the anxiety and stress you might feel about finding your purpose in life originate in false doctrines. We refer to these distorted doctrines as heresies. That may seem like a strong word, but it's fitting, because if you embrace these worldly doctrines, they will lead you far afield from how the Lord intends you to view your purpose in life. The heresies are precisely what bring you anxiety and threaten your sense of peace. But, if you embrace true principles rooted in the restored gospel to dispel these heresies, then you can replace anxiety with faith and hope.

In the remaining chapters, we will examine seven heresies about work. This is not an exhaustive list, but it represents those that seem to trouble our students the most. The seven great heresies we wish to dispel are the following:

Heresy #1: *Only lucky people find a calling in life.*

Heresy #2: *You only have one true calling in life.*

Heresy #3: *You get to choose your calling in life.*

Heresy #4: *You have to set aside your calling in order to support your family.*

Heresy #5: *When you find your calling, work will be blissful.*

Heresy #6: *When you find your calling, the world will take notice.*

Heresy #7: *Meaningfulness is found at work.*

It is not necessary to read these chapters in order. We welcome you to follow your nose to the heresies you think are most affecting you.

Endnotes

1. Monson, T. S. 1985. *Favorite Quotations from the Collection of Thomas S. Monson.* Salt Lake City: Deseret Books.
2. Luther, M. 1522. Sermon in the Castle Church at Weimar in *D. Martin Luthers Werke: Kritische Gesamtausgabe,* Herman Böhlaus Nachfolger.
3. Hardy, L. 1990. *The Fabric of This World: Inquiries into Calling, Career Choice, and the Design of Human Work.* William B. Eerdmans Publishing, page 48.
4. Quoted in Hardy, 1990, *The Fabric of This World,* page 62; also in *Sermons of M. John Calvin upon the Epistle of Saint Paul to the Galatians.* Lucas Harison and George Bishop, 1574], page 307; translation modified
5. Weber, M. 2003. *The Protestant Ethic and the Spirit of Capitalism,* translated by Talcott Parsons. Dover, page 182
6. Kohn, A. 1999. *Punished by Rewards: The Trouble with Gold Stars, Incentive Plans, A's, Praise, and Other Bribes.* Mariner Books.
7. See Elder David A. Bednar's talk entitled "The Tender Mercies of the Lord" in April 2005 General Conference report.
8. Lund, G. N. 2010. *Divine Signatures: The Confirming Hand of God.* Deseret Book.

Notes

CHAPTER 3

Who Gets a Calling?

**CORRECTING HERESY #1:
"ONLY LUCKY PEOPLE FIND A CALLING IN LIFE"**

April sits on the edge of the chair in her professor's office. She is twisting a Kleenex in her hand, hoping that she won't start crying again. She is a few months away from graduation in her Master's program. She has changed her emphasis twice already. Unlike many of her classmates, she has no job leads. She doesn't even really know what kind of a job she wants. Choking back the emotion, she speaks to her professor.

"My parents have sacrificed so much for me to get this degree. And I have put so much work into it. But now that I'm close to the end, I'm still questioning whether this is even what I was supposed to do. I've enjoyed some of my classes a lot. But others didn't interest me at all. And now that it's almost time to start my career, I don't even know what kind of work I would like to do. I'm scared. What if I end up in a job I hate? What if I missed the path that would give me the opportunity to be a wife and mother?

"Professor, I think about all the people you described who found their passion—doctors, teachers, zookeepers, artists. I love those stories. But I have never felt drawn to a particular profession like that. I don't have any remarkable talents. I just think that… maybe I'm not one of those people that even has a calling in life. And I'm really sad and confused about it."

For every kid who grows up knowing she was born to be a zookeeper (or some other distinctive occupation), there are probably a dozen Aprils. The idea of a calling in life might make the Aprils of the world feel they are deficient because they don't have a noticeable brilliant talent or some euphoric passion. But the belief that callings only happen to extraordinary people is one of the biggest heresies about work. Where does it leave us run-of-the-mill people who weren't born with crystal clarity about what we want to do?

A Good Cause

The first heresy we want to dispel is "only lucky people find a calling in life." Motivational speakers might not express the first heresy quite that blatantly. But, it's sort of implied in the motivational messages that dominate graduation speeches and self-help books today. You are told to "follow your passion." That's a nice enough sentiment. But it indirectly suggests that if you don't have some burning quest, there must be something wrong with you.

Can restored gospel principles help us dispel this heresy, and reassure us that callings aren't reserved only for the lucky and brilliant? Let's look at a wonderful scripture about life callings. You have probably read it many times, but perhaps you never considered its professional implications. In D&C 58, the Lord instructs His people to avoid slothfulness. And then in verse 27, he issues a stunning charge to us to "be anxiously engaged in a good cause, and do many things of [our] own free will and choice, and bring to pass much righteousness."

Let that sink in for a moment. The Lord doesn't issue this commandment only to the ultra-talented, but to people in general—to you. He tells you to pursue a good cause, but he *doesn't* dictate what that cause should be. In fact, he tells you that there are *many* things you could do, and that the cause you pursue is up to your "own free will and choice." This doesn't sound at all like the Lord expects you to have a single overriding passion that drives all of your life decisions. It also doesn't sound like you have to be extraordinary in order to contribute to good causes.

You might argue that "anxiously engaged" refers to church service, not to one's working life. Are you sure about that? Would the Lord so pointedly command you to be *anxiously* engaged in good causes, then give you a "pass" on the huge portion of your waking hours—8am to 5pm, for instance—during which you simply punch the metaphorical clock? The Lord is asking you to do *many* things in service to good causes. Why should your work not be one of them?

Let's return to Martin Luther for a moment. Recall his teaching that any kind of work can be a calling, as long as it benefits God's children. It's easy to think of medical researchers, special education teachers, and humanitarians as people who benefit others in important ways. But what about cubicle workers who spend their days filling out reports? What about food service workers? Custodians? Toll booth attendants? Can these jobs be a calling? According to the world's definition, probably not. But according to the Lord's standard in D&C 58, it all depends on the *cause* for which the person is doing the work. Even if you are doing the most mundane, unglamorous work, you are meeting the Lord's standard if your efforts are devoted to a good cause that serves His children.

The story of a young man named Nick drives this point home. When we met Nick, he was a young, impressive college student who could probably land any number of corporate jobs. But Nick's aspirations didn't run in that direction. All Nick wanted to do was the same thing he had been doing for years: serve pizza at his family's restaurant. Why would someone choose food service, of all things, if he could do any work he wanted? The reason is that Nick's work—which many people would consider menial—represented a cause for him.

Nick described his work as follows:

> "I love what I do. People come to our restaurant to celebrate, to be with each other, to have a good time. When I serve a great pizza, it's a memory-making moment. It makes me really happy. Nothing satisfies me more than helping family and friends make memories together."

Nick's is a moving testimonial. He doesn't just serve pizza; he is anxiously engaged in a good cause. You can find a lot of food service workers who are bitter and impatient. But you may also remember a waiter or waitress who made a meal memorable for you. If so, it was probably because they were thinking about serving *you*, not just serving food.

Another compelling food-service example shows up in Studs Terkel's book *Working*. Terkel interviewed a waitress named Dolores Dante who considered herself an artist in her work. Here are some excerpts:

> "I have to be a waitress. How else can I learn about people? How else does the world come to me? I can't go to everyone. So they have to come to me. Everyone wants to eat, everyone has hunger. And I serve them...

> "I can't be servile. I give service. There's a difference...

> "I don't give anything away. I just give myself... I'd get intoxicated with giving service."[1]

You have probably experienced the profound difference that an attitude like Nick's and Delores' can make. At the university where Stuart works, there used to be a small deli. The people behind the counter tended to be curt and impatient. Then the deli hired Jerome, who somehow hadn't gotten the memo that his job was boring, meaningless, and servile. He greeted every customer with a smile and a hearty "How's your day?"—a question that he persisted in asking until he got an answer. He remembered names and details about his customers.

At first, Jerome's in-your-face friendliness was a bit unnerving. But it didn't take long before people began to seek Jerome out. They walked out of his deli with a smile and a good word, not just a sandwich. When Jerome left, the faculty and students organized an event to bid him farewell.

So what can April learn from all this? First off, she needs to let go of the idea that callings only come to special people. She might not discover a single grand passion that makes her career a joyride (and we'll later argue that the joyride idea is also a heresy). But this doesn't mean that April has no calling. She most definitely has one, and it comes from her Heavenly Father. Her calling is to pour her heart into good causes and bring about righteousness by serving others. It's your calling too.

The Power Is In Us

April probably wouldn't be fully satisfied with our response yet. Although it's reassuring to know that Heavenly Father has a use for all of us, it doesn't tell April what sort of life she should lead, or how to land the right job.

D&C 58 helps here as well. Verse 27, about being "anxiously engaged," is a very popular verse. But for some reason, people rarely talk about the next verse, which expands on the doctrine the Lord is teaching. The beginning of verse 28 is glorious! After instructing his children to be anxiously engaged in a good cause, the Lord promises, "For the power is in them."

Now let that sink in. The Lord hasn't just told you to go out and pursue good causes. He has also equipped you with the *power* to do so. He has instilled in you divine capabilities—many still undiscovered—that will help you serve in meaningful ways. April doesn't need to worry about whether she is good enough. She doesn't need to fret that she'll accidentally miss out on her only opportunity to find a happy, complete life. She might be a little uncertain about her future path, but the fact is that she is a dynamo of divinely-appointed powers, which are just waiting to reveal themselves as April gets into action.

We will spend the next chapter talking about how April can discover the power that is in her (otherwise known as spiritual gifts). But for now, let's consider what we know about the Lord's expectations when He gives us gifts and powers.

Jesus used an intriguing parable to teach the principle of stewardship. It's about a man bound for a long journey who entrusts "talents" to three other men while he is away. He expects that they will invest and expand the value of the talents. The word "talent" in the New Testament most likely refers to a very large weight of silver. Some estimate a talent to be equivalent to the value of about 20 years of work by the average person in Jesus' time, so it is an extremely large amount. Of course, Jesus wasn't really teaching about financial investments here, but about God-given gifts. The fact that "talent" can refer to both a unit of currency and a spiritual gift is a happy, and probably not coincidental, convenience.

In the Matthew version of the parable, the investor (who represents the Lord) didn't distribute his talents equally among the three stewards—a significant insight in itself. But he expected each of them to apply their talents to earn even more. The stewards who received five and two talents both doubled their allotment. The investor was just as pleased with the man who returned four talents as he who returned ten—each doubled his investment. But the third steward, who had received only one talent, had hidden his up in the earth and returned it to his master with no increase at all. Asked to give an account of his actions, he replied, "I was afraid, and went and hid thy talent in the earth: lo, there thou hast that is thine" (Matthew 25:25). Of course, simply returning the original amount back to the investor was not dutiful at all. The investor condemns the steward because he expected an *increase*, just as the Lord does from us.

We don't mean to be too hard on April, who is honestly confused and trying to do the right thing. But do you see any parallels between her and the unwise steward who hid his talent? April, of course, has every intention of being a good person and rendering serving. But she has convinced herself that she isn't remarkably gifted (or in other words, she has only one talent compared to the five her peers seem to have). She has perhaps allowed herself to fade into the background in some of her more challenging classes, and has been a little too timid to go after job opportunities with the same gusto as her peers. And now, sitting in her professor's office, she admits that fear is paralyzing her, just as it did the unrighteous steward.

We have great sympathy for April, because we have been in her shoes before. In fact, if you apply the parable of the talents to your own life, you are probably like her sometimes as well. Do you sometimes slink into the shadows with fear rather than boldly employ the gifts you have been given?

Fear is one of the primary tools that the adversary uses to prevent God's children from using their gifts to serve. And fear is a dead giveaway that you are buying into the heresy that callings are reserved for the lucky or the brilliant.

Ironically, the heresy that callings are a matter of luck actually cuts both ways. It tends to paralyze both the less gifted *and* the more gifted. The reasons are both psychological and spiritual, and have everything to do with competition.

When you *compete* to be the most gifted, you focus on comparing yourself with others. Of course, the less gifted people fear inadequacy when they compare themselves to others with greater gifts. So, competition creates "fear at the bottom." April's story is a good example of how the fear of giftlessness might paralyze you. Let's examine a more surprising fear: the "fear at the top"—the fear of your own giftedness.

Fear of Our Own Gifts

Marcus (not his real name) is a young man who went back to school after working a few years to earn a Master's degree in the program where Jeff teaches at BYU. He is a truly imposing figure. A former college athlete, he is large, confident, and passionate. His personality is as big as his stature. People like him, and they always know when he is in the room. You just can't miss him.

Marcus had to overcome a great deal to get where he is in life, however. He grew up under trying family circumstances, and became involved with the gang culture in the large city where he grew up. His adolescent years were filled with violence. He witnessed, and even participated in, horrific beatings. Through turning to the Lord, however, Marcus got his life in order, served a faithful full-time mission, and became a sterling citizen. Today, he practically oozes faithfulness and natural leadership.

This is why everyone was so puzzled that Marcus always seemed to hold back in class, and to adopt a passive role on his team. It was as if he was always falling just short of putting his heart into his work or his relationships at school. This disappointed his classmates and teachers, who sensed that Marcus wasn't fulfilling his potential.

One day Marcus came to speak to Jeff in his office. Reflecting on his participation at school, he revealed the source of his hesitancy. This is what he said:

> *"I have realized that, with my large stature and my loud voice, I can easily dominate other people. I spent so much of my life bullying people to get my way. I don't want to be the kind of person that dictates out of force. So I've really been trying to keep my mouth*

shut and to stay in the background when I'm around my teammates. I'm afraid I'm going to overpower them if I don't."

On the one hand, Marcus was showing remarkable sensitivity with these insights. He recognized that he still has within him the potential to dominate and bully, and he is doing his best to avoid past sins.

On the other hand, Marcus' fears are tragic. "What a waste of a natural gift!," Jeff thought. Marcus is the kind of person that can energize and inspire other people. His stature and his strong voice could be great assets to help him influence and serve other people. And yet he was burying that gift in the ground, like the unwise steward, because of fear.

Marcus' story reminds us of a brilliant quote that is often misattributed to Nelson Mandela, who used it in one of his great speeches. The original author is Marianne Williamson. You may have read it before, but it merits frequent pondering:

"Our deepest fear is not that we are inadequate. Our deepest fear is that we are powerful beyond measure. It is our light, not our darkness that most frightens us. We ask ourselves, 'Who am I to be brilliant, gorgeous, talented, fabulous?' Actually, who are you not to be? You are a child of God. Your playing small does not serve the world. There is nothing enlightened about shrinking so that other people won't feel insecure around you. We are all meant to shine, as children do. We were born to make manifest the glory of God that is within us. It's not just in some of us; it's in everyone. And as we let our own light shine, we unconsciously give other people permission to do the same. As we are liberated from our own fear, our presence automatically liberates others."[2]

Marcus has figured out that his gift for influence is dangerous if he uses it self-servingly. Now he needs to discover that it will be glorious when he uses it to serve others. That's true of virtually any of the millions of human talents you might be blessed with. They can all be used for ill or for good. That's why the Lord instructed you to make sure that you choose "a good cause."

So, which of your gifts are you suppressing so that others won't feel awkward around you? Do you fear your own innate greatness? Is this fear keeping your from recognizing your calling in life? If you reflect on the ways you may have chosen to fade into the background, to worry about others' perceptions of you, or to pass up a chance to speak out about something important, then you might start to better understand the unwise servant who buried his talent. There are dozens of ways that you can "play small," justifying it as modesty. Jesus' words for that were "putting your candle under a bushel" (see Matthew 5:15).

But misplaced modesty isn't the only way that the heresy of lucky callings discourages the gifted. It damages us even more through pride. Some surprising research in the field of psychology suggests that pride is very closely linked with—of all things—fear. You might assume that arrogant people are immune to criticism and outrageously confident in their abilities. But research by psychologist Carol Dweck and her colleagues reveals that arrogance is a thin façade for many people who are actually very insecure.

Dweck's research has looked at the difference between people who believe that talents and intelligence can be acquired versus those who believe talents and intelligence are inborn and unchangeable (the latter is basically a version of the heresy that callings are for the lucky). It turns out that this basic belief makes a dramatic difference in almost every aspect of our lives. People who believe that talents are fixed and unchangeable have the following characteristics:

- They avoid trying new activities
- They avoid new information, sticking instead to what they know

- They avoid receiving feedback
- They compare themselves only to less talented people (to make themselves feel better), rather than learning from more talented people
- They reduce their effort after experiencing a failure, and are more prone to depression

The list of bad outcomes for the belief in fixed talents goes on and on. And in every case, the polar opposite is true for people who fundamentally believe that you can develop talents through hard work. They are more open to new experiences, more receptive to feedback, more inclined to learn from others, and more resilient after failure.[3]

Perhaps most important, though, is the finding that people who believe their talents are fixed put in far *less* effort than their counterparts who believe talents can be developed. Dweck uses many examples to illustrate this, including prima donna athletes who are lackadaisical on the practice field. While it might look like these people are simply arrogant in their refusal to practice, her research suggests that it's actually the *fear of failure* that keeps them from practicing hard. "After all," they distortedly reason, "if I have to practice hard, then that means I'm not talented after all. And if people start to think that I'm not naturally talented, then I'm nothing." These are the fruits of the heresy of lucky callings: it tends to paralyze the most gifted.

The great news from Dweck's research is that your belief about the nature of talent turns out to be a choice. You can develop a healthier approach to work and to life in general if you catch yourself when you say things like, "I'm just no good at this" or "I could never be as smart as she is." A boatload of research shows that people who focus on effort improve their performance far more quickly in almost any endeavor than people who focus on whether they have talent or not.

This principle has important applications for parenting as well. If you view talents as fixed, even the way you *praise* your children might cause some damage. For instance, if you constantly say, "You are so smart!" or "You are so talented!," you may unwittingly cause your children to think that inborn gifts are the only thing they have going for them. When they fail, as all of us inevitably do, it might rock their self-concept—"My dad always said I'm smart, but if I fail, then maybe he was wrong. I had better just do easy stuff so that people won't find out I'm not smart after all." Dweck suggests that you should praise your children more for their *effort* than for their innate abilities. After a piano recital, you might say to your daughter, "Look how your hard work paid off! You really know how to practice, honey. I'm really proud of you. You can do anything you want to if you work hard enough."

Getting Unstuck from Fear

So, what advice should we give April, and all of the other people who feel paralyzed because of uncertainty and fear that they won't find their calling in life? The first thing April needs to do is recognize and root out the false doctrine that she is buying into. The romanticized worldly version of callings has led her to believe that she might have gotten the short end of the stick when the Lord was distributing talents. Or maybe, even if she *was* one of the five-talent recipients, she won't be smart enough, or in tune enough, to use them well.

All of this is utterly wrong.

April doesn't need to be afraid that she lacks special gifts. Once she fully accepts that she is a daughter of God, she can exercise faith to know that she is unique, and precious beyond price. There is no need for her to fear that the Lord has forgotten her. The only thing that should frighten her is *not doing anything*, which is what the one-talent steward did (and what she herself has been doing).

Remember that April has, after all, chosen a path (in her case, a degree), and she has done so prayerfully. That path may not be turning out exactly as she thought it would. But the parable of the talents suggests that, even so, she should still be making the very most of her experience while she is on that path. Even if it's not a perfect path, there are things for her to learn while she is on it. If and when the time comes that she should switch course and take another path, the Spirit will help her to know it, and the Lord will open the right doors. But if she simply coasts by, waiting for something to happen, she will miss the opportunity to expand her gifts.

April's reaction calls to mind an experience that Stuart had with his oldest daughter Joslyn when she was about four years old. They were playing with a small ball on the second-story back porch of their home. The ball bounced over the railing and down into the lawn below. They peered together over the railing and saw the ball nestled in the tall grass (the lawn was far overdue for mowing). Joslyn ran down the stairs to get the ball while Stuart watched from his position on the porch. But when she got down to the lawn, she could no longer see the ball because of the height of the grass. She called up to ask her daddy where the ball was. He told her that as she walked nearer the ball, he would call out "warmer" and as she got further away, he would call out "colder." After wandering around the lawn for five minutes or so without finding the ball, Joslyn grew frustrated. Finally, she stopped walking, stamped her foot, and called up to the porch, "Just tell me if I am hotter or colder!" Stuart truly wanted to help her, but there was no way to respond to her request. He couldn't tell her if she was hotter or colder unless she was moving ... but she was standing still.

We often act like Stuart's little daughter as we search for our path in life. We are in tall grass and are impatient to find the ball. Fortunately, your Father in Heaven sees your landscape clearly, and will help you find your way by means of the "warmer" and "colder" promptings that come through the Holy Spirit. But the Holy Spirit can't tell you if you are getting warmer or colder unless you are moving.

As April stalls, waiting for clarity *before* she pours her heart into her current endeavor, she is actually limiting Heavenly Father's ability to guide her. She is much like a car stuck in neutral that is waiting for the steering wheel to take it to a good destination. Only when you are *moving* can the Lord steer you.

Are you in the same situation as April? Do you sometimes fear that you aren't special enough to have a calling in life? Do you find yourself immobilized by questioning and doubt? There is absolutely nothing wrong with questioning what your gifts are, and whether you are on the right path. But there *is* something wrong with allowing fear to paralyze you professionally or personally. Stopping and waiting by the side of the path is good advice if you have lost your way in the wilderness and you know a search party will be looking for you, but it is terrible advice for people searching for a path to their calling. It is only through moving forward—trying things out, experimenting, attempting to serve (however inept we may feel)—that you discover what cause you can anxiously engage yourself in.

In coming chapters, we will have more concrete advice for April and people who, like her, are feeling stuck in uncertainty about their professional paths. To conclude our discussion of the first heresy, however, we strongly encourage you to engage in the following activities. Taking time for each of these thought experiments will invite the Spirit to give you personalized direction that is far more tailored to you than anything you could read in a book like this. So please find a quiet space, and do the following:

What To Do Now

1. Find a notebook or journal that you can use to record reflections as you work through the exercises in this book. Elder Richard G. Scott has taught powerfully that you are most likely to receive personal revelation when you ponder deeply and commit your thoughts to

writing (see April 2012 General Conference talk). Don't skimp on this part of the process!

2. Imagine that you have just come home and found a large important-looking envelope in your mailbox. When you open it, you discover that it's a certified letter from a law firm. It informs you that you have a long-lost aunt who recently passed away, leaving no immediate descendants. As the next of kin, you stand to inherit her entire fortune—hundreds of millions of dollars. It's enough money that you will never have to work another day in your life if you don't want to. However, your aunt was an eccentric who left an unusual stipulation on the inheritance. You will only receive the inheritance if you commit *right now* to a life work that you will pursue until you die. And you have only 5 minutes to make that decision.

3. Spend 5 minutes generating (and writing in your journal) a list of pursuits you would be willing to do for the rest of your life if money were no object. Be as creative and fanciful as you like! Nothing is too outrageous.

4. As the 5 minutes draws to a close, choose your top idea as if you were about to call the law firm and make your commitment.

5. (Alternative to activity #2) If the inheritance activity didn't really click for you, instead make a list of the "causes" you care about. You can generate a list of causes by thinking about the following questions:

- What types of projects would you be willing to volunteer for, without the possibility of pay?
- What types of media stories catch your attention?
- Under what circumstances do you tend to feel strong emotions about other people's needs?

6. Review the list that you generated in Activity #2 and/or 3. Ponder about what the list tells you about yourself. Did an "easy" answer leap immediately to your mind? Or was the task difficult? Are there commonalities among the themes you wrote? Although some of the items may be far-fetched, scratch below the surface to think about underlying themes behind your ideas. Write your reflections in your journal.

7. If you currently have a job, think about needs that are currently not being met there, or problems that need to be solved. If you don't have a job, think about a need or problem in some organization you are associated with (including family, church, or social groups). The needs you identify might be directly related to the business of your organization, or they might involve personal needs that your associates have. Make a list of these needs. Then identify the one that you think you are best equipped to help with. Make and implement a plan to try to serve that particular need in some way this week. Afterwards, record what you did and reflect on what it reveals about causes that excite you.

8. Start making a list of your professional and personal fears. Be as inclusive as you can. Ask yourself which of these fears come from a belief that you lack a talent and can't develop it, or perhaps the belief that you shouldn't reveal a talent that you have. Ask yourself which of your fears represent "putting your candle under a bushel." Make a plan to confront one of those fears this week. Seek Heavenly Father's help through prayer to have the courage to step outside of your comfort zone.

Endnotes

1. Terkel, S. 1972. *Working: People Talk About What They Do All Day and How They Feel About What They Do*. The New Press. Page 294–296.

2. Williamson, M. 1992. *A Return to Love: Reflections on the Principles of a Course in Miracles.* Harper Collins. Page 190–191.
3. For an accessible and fascinating account of this research, see Dweck, C. 2001. *Mindset: The New Psychology of Success.* Ballantine Books.

Notes

CHAPTER 4

Spiritual Gifts and Callings

**CORRECTING HERESY #2:
"YOU ONLY HAVE ONE TRUE CALLING IN LIFE"**

Stuart recently visited his daughter's third-grade class as the "Mystery Reader" for the week. As he waited outside the classroom for his surprise entrance, he passed the time reading the short autobiographies the students had posted on the outside wall. The teacher had assigned each student to talk about who they are—their family, their siblings, their likes and dislikes, and what they were good at. Stuart was struck by how open and confident the students were about their individual gifts. They said things like: "I am really good at helping my Mom and Dad," "I play the piano really well," or "I am a great artist." It was fun for him to see these eight and nine year-olds discovering and articulating their unique gifts and talents. He had to chuckle at what his daughter had written: "I am really good at basketball. My team was really good and scored lots of baskets." She really did give her heart and soul to that team. But they lost most of their games. And she never scored a single basket. Skill had not quite caught up with passion when it came to that particular "gift."

The doctrine of spiritual gifts lies at the very core of what it means to experience a calling. A calling, as we noted earlier, is where your gifts meet the world's need. You can't really discover your calling, then, without first understanding your gifts.

The doctrine of spiritual gifts is clearly very important in the gospel. There are detailed discussions of spiritual gifts in the New Testament, in the Book of Mormon, and in the Doctrine and Covenants. A belief in spiritual gifts is one of the thirteen Articles of Faith. Moroni took up precious space on the plates in his concluding writings to teach about spiritual gifts. Both Mormon and Moroni lamented those who deny spiritual gifts, suggesting that they must not understand the scriptures or the gospel of Christ (Mor. 9:7–8; 3 Ne. 29:6). As Paul explained to the Corinthians, "Now concerning spiritual gifts, brethren, I would not have you ignorant" (1 Cor. 12:1). And as the Lord revealed to Joseph Smith, "And again, verily I say unto you, I would that ye should always remember, and always retain in your minds what those gifts are, that are given unto the church."

If spiritual gifts are such an important part of your mortal experience, it is no wonder that you started at an early age to try to define what you are good at. As you got older, you might have begun to worry about finding your *one* great gift so that you knew exactly what you are meant to do with your life. What if you miss your calling in life because you never figure out what your one great gift is?

That is an anxiety-inducing question! But the doctrine of spiritual gifts is not meant to make us anxious; it is a beautiful, hopeful doctrine. Sometimes, however, we lose the hopefulness and fall prey to the second heresy we would like to dispel. That heresy, which the world often perpetuates, is that you have to find your *one* true calling in life in order to be fulfilled.

This heresy should remind you of your favorite fairy tale, in which the princess finds her "one true love." People seem to prefer those tidy endings where everything works out exactly as it is supposed to. But does Heavenly Father's plan for your life include perfect fits and predestined destinations? The doctrine of spiritual gifts teaches a lot about those questions.

A Diversity of Gifts

The scriptures make it clear that spiritual gifts take many different forms. Paul observes that "there are diversities of gifts" (1 Cor. 12: 4). Moroni said simply, "there are many" (Moroni 10:8). The seventh article of faith provides examples of spiritual gifts, and then notably concludes with "and so forth," suggesting that the list could go on and on. And Elder Bruce R. McConkie said that "spiritual gifts are endless in number and infinite in variety."[1] Scriptural examples of spiritual gifts include wisdom, knowledge, teaching, faith, healing, speaking in tongues, the interpretation of tongues, and administration. But these represent a sampling, and not an exhaustive list. Surely, as part of the infinite variety of spiritual gifts, we should also list gifts like: hand-eye coordination, wit and humor, mechanical logic, public speaking, powers of observation, spatial perspective, a green thumb, critical analysis, a willing heart, tolerance for discomfort, perfect pitch, a love of history, athletic prowess, abstract thinking, project management, complimenting others, and creating order. We could continue with the list until this book is full, but we still wouldn't have scratched the surface on the ways in which Heavenly Father equips us to serve each other. Spiritual gifts indeed come in *all* shapes and sizes.

Sometimes the size seems very small indeed. Stuart's wife, Maren, was at a family gathering some time ago with her grandmother, who was 85 years old. After a meal, Grandma got up to sweep the floor. Maren urged her to sit down and rest and let others take care of that simple chore. Her grandmother responded, "Please let me do it. I'm really good at sweeping. This is how I can help."

Sweeping a floor may not make most people's list of great spiritual gifts. But Maren's grandmother knew instinctively that she was equipped to help in that way. She wanted to use her simple talent to bless others. And there is the dead giveaway! Your gifts are your instinctive responses to other people's needs. Gifts reveal themselves *as you serve.*

What Gifts Are For

Latter-day scripture teaches that spiritual gifts "are given for the benefit of those who love me… that all may be benefited" (DC 46: 9). They exist so that "all may be profited thereby" (DC 46: 12). We human beings can experience an almost endless number of needs. So, it shouldn't be surprising that the Lord has equipped his children with an endless assortment of gifts. There are at least as many spiritual gifts in the world as there are human needs, because that is the point of a gift: to serve another's need.

The world tends to get pretty mixed up on this one. People usually talk about gifts as if they glorify the possessor. When you hear someone say, "She is so gifted," you might sense an undercurrent of jealousy. Sadly, many people do strive primarily for self-gratification, prestige, or personal enrichment through their talents. But your Father in Heaven is very clear that spiritual gifts are for serving, not "that they might consume it upon their lusts" (DC 46:9). Notice the shift in mindset: A gift is not something you have been given, it's something that allows you to give.

Our friend Bob Chapman is a wonderful example of this principle. Bob is the second-generation CEO of a company in St. Louis called Barry-Wehmiller. He became CEO at the tender age of 29 with the untimely passing of his father. Bob spent the first 15 years of his tenure as CEO applying the principles he learned in his MBA program to improve the health of the family business. He streamlined operations, expanded the company through acquisition, and imposed sound fiscal discipline. The results were spectacular. But something was missing. Bob felt empty.

One day, Bob was observing a wedding in his church. He watched as the minister placed the hand of the bride in the hand of the groom. He reflected on the feelings of that bride's parents and family, their hopes and prayers that this young man would love their daughter as they did, cherish and respect her the way they would. It suddenly struck him that he had a similar responsibility with each employee who was placed in his care. Each had loved ones who hoped that the company would treat their son, daughter, brother, sister, father, or mother with respect and dignity. They were, in a sense, placing the hand of their loved one in Bob's care and hoping that he would honor that responsibility. He began to think very differently about his work. He began to recognize that the gifts he had been given—the ownership and management of the company, his skills and education as a manager—meant that he had a responsibility to those employees.

This basic insight led to a cultural revolution at Barry-Wehmiller. The company's mission, and Bob's private, all-consuming passion, is now centered on "truly human leadership." He has become an evangelist for these principles throughout corporate America.

We once asked Bob if he felt that this focus on truly human leadership was a calling for him. His response was inspiring: "I have been called to reaffirm the way the world was intended to be: a society where we think of others first, where everyone matters. Do I feel a calling? YES! And that is what drives me."

Bob's calling affects the lives of thousands. But as the story of the grandmother with the broom illustrates, spiritual gifts don't have to be grandiose and far-reaching. Some are supremely humble. And yet, if we diminish their significance, we fundamentally misunderstand the nature of spiritual gifts.

Finding Your Spiritual Gifts

Faced with an almost infinite array of possibilities, how do you go about discovering what *your* gifts are? Just like the third graders listing their talents in their biographies, a lot of it is guesswork in the beginning. You may find your gifts haphazardly, in the midst of self-doubts and surprises, second-guessing and sudden epiphanies. You usually have to exercise faith and perseverance before they become obvious to you.

Developing faith in your spiritual gifts is difficult if you are lending an ear to the second heresy, which tells you there is one "right" path. So, a prerequisite for discovering your gifts is to turn a deaf ear to the heresy and attune yourself instead to these principles:

1. Refuse to compare your gifts with others'

Other people's gifts can inspire and bless us. But sometimes, instead of feeling gratitude for others' talents, we compare them to our own deficiencies and become paralyzed by feelings of inadequacy. Jealousy and self-abasement prevent us from finding a sense of purpose in life.

We observed one of the consequences of comparing gifts in the experience of a fellow professor who lacked self-confidence as an instructor. He had long idolized a senior faculty member in his department, and decided to try to emulate him in every way. Students began chuckling behind his back, though, as they noticed that this professor was adopting the same quirky mannerisms and speech patterns as the senior professor he admired. The students found him inauthentic. Only years later did this young professor finally discover his own authentic style in the classroom. Trying to replicate others' gifts reminds us of a quote by Bob Goff at the 2013 Global Leadership Summit: "Don't live someone else's calling; it will come off like a bad Elvis impression."

The Savior's words to Peter at the Sea of Galilee after His crucifixion emphasize this principle. In that conversation, Jesus told Peter he would have the honor and challenge of being martyred for his faith. He

Spiritual Gifts and Callings

then re-issued the invitation: "Follow me." We can only imagine how Peter must have felt. He was probably frightened. He clearly wondered if he was the only one who would be asked to die in this way. Peter turned to the Savior and asked what would happen to his friend and companion, John. Jesus responded: "If I will that he tarry till I come, what is that to thee? Follow thou me" (John 21:22). The Savior thus taught Peter that John had another path—a path that did not include painful martyrdom but that undoubtedly had its own unique challenges. He seemed to want Peter to avoid wasting energy comparing his own path with John's. Peter's charge was to follow the Savior and be true to the calling that he had been given, without comparing his calling to another's. We should do the same.

2. Recognize that God will use your various gifts at different times in your life

Some people are interested in almost everything, and good at many things. If that's true of you, then you might struggle to find one focus that feels right. This was Greg's problem. Greg was a smart, talented, and disciplined child. He was an energetic boy who loved the outdoors, relished Scouting, and had a strong sense of patriotism and civic duty. Clearly, he had many gifts and therefore many options when it came time to choose a profession. At the urging of teachers and family, he trained as a lawyer and, not surprisingly, became very successful at it. He achieved a prominent position in a government agency.

But Greg was never completely happy in his work. He felt something was missing. He had always dreamed of serving his country in law enforcement or the military, but he had been so focused on developing his legal skills that he had put this other dream on the shelf. When we met him, he felt he was simply too old to think about making a change.

Then, some unexpected complications arose at work and Greg found himself out of a job, and with a bad taste in his mouth about

CALLING

the profession to which he had devoted his life. What's more, he found that he could muster no enthusiasm for pursuing another job in law or government. At his age, any options in law enforcement or the military seemed closed. He looked at opportunities in border control, but the entry requirements—particularly the intensive physical screening—seemed an insurmountable obstacle.

After wandering for a while, Greg finally decided that he would never forgive himself if he did not at least try. So he applied to be a border control agent. The application process alone was difficult. And then he had to endure a grueling "boot camp" in which he was forced to compete with men who were more than 15 years his junior. Once again, Greg drew on his gifts in order to succeed—his determination, his sense of patriotism, his endurance, his positive outlook. He pushed himself beyond what he thought he could ever do, even breaking his leg at one point. In the end, he was selected, the oldest recruit in his group. Several months later, he moved his wife and family and began his new adventure. He has loved his new position and has never looked back.

Greg's particular talents and abilities made it possible for him to pursue two very different career paths. He rendered valuable service in both. But in the end, his persistence and his courage allowed him the opportunity to pursue both at different points in his life. Having "too many gifts" didn't paralyze Greg with indecision. He simply pursued a reasonable one until life, and the Spirit, propelled him in another direction.

3. Seek to develop new spiritual gifts

The scriptures clearly teach us to develop *new* gifts. We are, in fact, commanded to "seek earnestly the best gifts, always remembering for what they are given" (D&C 46: 8; see also 1 Cor. 12: 31).

The experience of a sister missionary named Christine illustrates this point. Christine felt that she was poor at learning new languages.

She worked hard in her high school Spanish class, but never made much progress. Several years later, she was called to serve a mission in Ecuador. Not long after receiving her call, she happened to run into her high school Spanish teacher and mentioned that she would be serving as a missionary for her church in Ecuador. The teacher shook her head and said, "You were one of my all-time favorite students. But you could not speak Spanish worth a darn."

But, like all missionaries who are called to learn a new language, Christine trusted in the inspiration behind her calling and began to "seek earnestly" the gift of tongues through hard work, study, and a lot of prayer. You know the result, because you probably know a missionary who has gone through something similar. Her hard work, dedication, and faith led to a small miracle—a manifestation of the gift of tongues. Christine may have had to work harder than others, but by seeking earnestly the best gifts with a desire to serve, something that was not a natural talent nonetheless became a spiritual gift.

Tools for Gift-Finding

Fortunately, there are powerful tools to assist you in discovering your spiritual gifts. In this section, we'll discuss a few of them, and then invite you to try using these tools to gain greater insights about your own gifts.

Revisit Childhood

One important tool for finding your gifts might surprise you: your own childhood. Recall in Chapter 1 that the zookeepers in our study believed that they were "hardwired" to work with animals. Most of them could point to childhood experiences that revealed their gift for caring for animals. They talked about bringing home lizards, bugs, and stray cats. They recalled reading about, talking about, and dreaming about animals.

Part of the magic of childhood is authenticity; Children explore what they love, and do things in a way that feels natural to them. Only later, when the expectations of others became important, do you start to question your interests, or to do things mostly to gain approval.

Many spiritual gifts manifest themselves early in life, just as they did with our zookeeper friends. Reflecting on your childhood activities is a generative way to remind yourself about how you are naturally gifted. Were you the kid who always got the neighborhood baseball game going? Maybe you have a spiritual gift for organizing others into collective action. Were you a natural storyteller? Maybe you have a spiritual gift for presenting ideas in a compelling and dramatic way. Were you the person who other kids always sought out for sympathy and acceptance? Maybe you have a spiritual gift for listening and discerning others' emotions.

One tricky thing about identifying your spiritual gifts is that they seem so natural to you. You may not even recognize them as gifts. You might think, "It wasn't a big deal that I organized the neighborhood baseball game. I just wanted to play baseball." You didn't think twice about taking the lead. But the fact is that you did lead out, and other kids didn't. There was something innate and special about your ability to pull people together. And even if you haven't organized a baseball game for decades, you still have within you that natural ability to bring people together. It's a more special trait than you probably give yourself credit for. This is true of almost anything that came natural to you in childhood.

When we ask people to think carefully about how their spiritual gifts manifested themselves in childhood, they are often surprised by what they remember. They gain insights about their gifts that had never occurred to them.

One of our favorite examples is Matt. As a young boy, his parents took him to Disneyland. He loved it, of course. But he loved it in a different way than you might expect. While others were thrilled by the rides and attractions, Matt was fascinated by the orderliness of the "village." He was awestruck that people had created a place that was so clean, so happy, and so organized. He returned home from the trip, and immediately began sketching out utopian communities (not your typical activity for a pre-teen!). He drew blueprint after blueprint, and only gave up his sketching when the demands of school and teenage life began to occupy most of his time.

It wasn't until years later, when we asked Matt to think about what he loved to do in childhood, that he recalled his childhood fascination with designing a utopia. It might be hard to believe, but Matt had never drawn a parallel between that experience and his current job: city planner! He had struggled for years, searching for a profession that suited him, before he found this job that he loved so much. But the clues had been there from the very beginning. Matt has a spiritual gift for designing communities, and the child within him knew it better than the adult did.

Ask Other People. Sometimes other people can see your spiritual gifts more clearly than you can. Once again, this is because your spiritual gifts feel so natural to you that you may not register them as unique. A fish may not appreciate the fact that it is a good swimmer—swimming is just what it does! Psychologists have called these gifts "unconscious competencies," things you are good at but remain unaware that you are good at. One of the best ways to identify your unconscious competencies is to seek feedback from those who know you well.

We often engage our students in an exercise designed to help them discover these unconscious competencies. It's called the *Reflected Best Self* exercise and was developed by scholars at the University of Michigan. The idea is simple. The participant identifies 10–20 people that have known her well throughout her life—parents, family members, bosses, coworkers, friends, coaches, piano teachers, school teachers, professors. She then asks these people to identify a few specific instances in which they saw her "at her very best." She doesn't ask them to elaborate about her strengths, or to say anything about her weaknesses. She just asks them to share a few brief stories. She then collects all of those stories, reads them, and looks for common themes. Those common themes often provide powerful and surprising insights about spiritual gifts.

One executive student with years of experience in marketing and public relations said the following about her experience with the exercise:

"The feedback, in addition to being a much needed ego boost, was extremely interesting and enlightening. Many of the skills people commented on were areas that, to me, did not seem particularly valuable, rather what should be expected, such as remaining calm during a crisis or stressful situation. Additionally, I was extremely surprised to see the consistency between the groups."

Consult Your Patriarchal Blessing

President (then Elder) Thomas S. Monson said that "a patriarchal blessing literally contains chapters from your book of eternal possibilities" (General Conference, October 1986). Many patriarchal blessings provide explicit insight into spiritual gifts. Others provide guidance and encouragement about how you can discover those gifts. And still others provide insight into the gifts that you should "seek earnestly" to develop in order to accomplish specific missions and purposes. As President Monson taught, "Your patriarchal blessing is to you a personal Liahona to chart your course and guide your way." It probably will not tell you to pursue a particular vocation, but almost all patriarchal blessings provide insight into your spiritual gifts.

Seek Divine Inspiration. Ultimately, the best and surest guide to gaining insight into your spiritual gifts is the guidance of the Holy Ghost. The Spirit guides you "into all truth" (John 16:13), and that certainly includes truth about yourself. As you ponder, record your thoughts, pray, read the scriptures, and attend the temple, you can gain insight into the gifts that you have or should seek to develop. Elder Robert D. Hales taught, " To find the gifts we have been given, we must pray and fast... I urge you each to discover your gifts and to seek after those that will bring direction to your life's work and that will further the work of heaven."[2]

But as we discussed in the previous chapter, simply asking the Lord to give you answers may not be sufficient. The Spirit is most likely to guide you into personal truth if you are also experimenting with potential pursuits, and then prayerfully pondering what you are learning in the process. Elder John H. Groberg of the Seventy taught this principle clearly:

"In the past, I have tried to figure out whether I should go into business or into teaching or into the arts or whatever. As I have begun to proceed along one path, having more or less gathered what facts I could, I have found that if that decision was wrong... without fail, the Lord has let me know just this emphatically: 'That is wrong. Do not go that way. That is not right for you.'

On the other hand there may have been two or three ways that I could have gone, any of which would have been right and would have been in the general area providing the experience and means whereby I could fulfill the mission that the Lord had in mind for me. Because he knows we need the growth, he generally does not point and say, 'Open that door and go twelve yards in that direction; then turn right and go two miles . . .' But if it is wrong, he will let us know—we will feel it for sure. I am positive of that.

So rather than saying, 'I will not move until I have this burning in my heart', let us turn it around and say, 'I will move unless I feel it is wrong... [V]ery quickly you will find yourself going in the direction that you ought to be going and then you can receive the assurance: 'Yes, I am going in the right direction. I am doing what my Father in Heaven wants me to do.'"[3]

Elder Groberg's words ring true to what we have learned about finding your spiritual gifts. When you make a decision and start moving, Heavenly Father can help you to know whether you are getting warmer or colder, just like Joslyn looking for the ball in the tall grass in Chapter 3. You will discover that some activities fit you like a glove, and then you can know that you have followed your gifts. Other activities will feel alien to you—not just hard, but in some way ill-fitting. It doesn't mean that the activity is a bad one. Rather, it might be the Spirit instructing you to focus instead on something that is more aligned with your spiritual gifts.

Be Specific

Lastly, one of the biggest barriers to discovering spiritual gifts is that people often don't undertake the effort to be *specific* about their gifts. They often allow themselves to talk in unhelpful generalities. For instance, we often encounter students who say things like, "I don't know what kind of work I should do. All I know is that I like working with people." That's a reasonable statement. But it doesn't even begin to explore one's spiritual gifts. It's actually a fairly lazy thing to say. When students give us the "I like working with people" line, we always respond by asking "How? There are millions of ways to work with people. What is *your* way? Are you gifted at challenging people to strive for their best? At exhibiting compassion when they are frustrated? At delivering constructive feedback? At creating enthusiasm? At teaching a complex principle? At telling stories that spellbind your listeners? At running a meeting?"

Can you see that there are countless ways to "work with people?"

In fact, "working with people" isn't a spiritual gift; it's a massive constellation of spiritual gifts. Until you get really specific about what it is that you have to offer, you won't make much progress at identifying spiritual gifts. No one has exactly your personality, your insights, your talents, your idiosyncrasies. You owe it to yourself, and to your Creator, to be more thoughtful about what you have to offer than just to say "I like working with people" (or any other general statement). So, as you undertake the pursuit of your calling, don't settle for easy answers. Continually push below the surface to the *specific* nature of your spiritual gifts.

Your Calling is Where Your Spiritual Gifts *Intersect*

We started off this chapter by warning you of the second heresy about callings: the false doctrine that you have to find your one true calling to be fulfilled. That really is an offensive doctrine. It grossly undervalues the glorious creation that you are. Do you really believe Heavenly Father created children that could only do one thing in life?

You are not a robot with a single worthwhile function, but an incredible, complex, magnificent combination of spiritual gifts, drawn from the "infinite" and "endless" variety of gifts that Elder McConkie spoke of. Your Father in Heaven intends to use your particular array of gifts in many different ways throughout your life. So instead of thinking about your calling in life as a specific job, role, or occupation, define your calling as a process of learning about and using your spiritual gifts, in whatever opportunities you are blessed with.

So, as a conclusion to this chapter, we want to suggest an alternative to the second heresy. Fulfillment in life doesn't come through finding your one true path. Rather, it comes from making connections between your variety of spiritual gifts, and using as much of that repertoire as you can to serve in unique ways.

CALLING

A story might help illustrate the point we want to make about combinations of gifts. Santiago Michalek is a young artist who is exceptionally gifted. But he is just one of countless talented young artists trying to make their mark on the world. Unfortunately, just having a talent for painting is not enough to give most artists the elusive opportunity for popular success. The same principle is probably true for you as well. You can't realistically hope to be the best in the world at something that a lot of other people also do.

But Santiago is not *just* an artist. He's also a passionate restorer of old Volkswagens. In fact, repairing and restoring VWs was how Santiago made a living to support his family while he honed his artistic skills. Spending countless hours dissecting and reassembling old VWs, he mastered their "anatomy" as thoroughly as he has mastered the anatomy of the human figures he draws. It was probably only natural, then, that Santiago started creating paintings of Volkswagens—usually battered old VW buses. That isn't typical subject matter for a fine artist. But when you look carefully at Santiago's work, you will notice that his VW paintings seem to caress the old cars with light, each dent and windshield reflection almost luminous. There is a dignity about the old beat-up cars he paints. In Santiago's work, the rusting hull of a ramshackle bus isn't a discarded relic, but a treasure worthy of restoration and revitalization—kind of like people who sometimes feel defeated by life. And to people who are quasi-religious in their devotion to old VWs, Santiago's art represents a truly unique contribution.

There are myriads of struggling artists in the world. And there are myriads of people who restore VWs. But as far as he knows, Santiago is the only artist who has combined these two spiritual gifts into a successful profession. You see, recently Santiago had to close up his VW restoration business. His artwork (particular his Volkswagen work) has become so successful that he can now support his family solely as an artist. The *intersection* of his gifts has led him to a truly unique calling in life.

Like Santiago, you usually don't discover your calling by figuring out what your *one* talent is. You discover your calling when you explore the intersection of your *various* talents. Like the innumerable combinations of DNA that make you unique, you have a mind-boggling complexity of gifts, abilities, interests, and viewpoints. Your combination of gifts is as unique in the history of the world as your fingerprint. There never has been and never again will be someone in the world who has your exact repertoire of gifts! The world needs that combination, and can't get it anywhere else but from you.

So if you feel like you are just one out of a million people who are trying to make your mark in life, competing against more talented people in a race to be excellent at one great thing, stop and take inventory of your spiritual gifts. What combination of gifts will allow you to do things—multiple things—in a *different way* than anyone else? If you are an accountant, what talents and abilities will make you a different flavor of accountant than anyone else? If you are a homemaker, how can you use your array of gifts to build a family in the way only you can? No painter is *just* a painter. Nobody is just vanilla.

To put the final nail in the coffin of the second heresy, we counsel you never to assume that there is only one true calling for you, and that you are a failure if you don't find it. Among all of Heavenly Father's creations, you are the most complex and multi-faceted. He can use your combination of gifts in many, many ways to serve His children. And He will no doubt use them differently during different stages of your life. You can dismiss the discouraging second heresy from your life by redefining calling. Your calling in life is not to find the perfect job. It is to use the repertoire of spiritual gifts that Heavenly Father has given you to serve others.

What To Do Now:

1. Review your patriarchal blessing. If you haven't received it, make a plan to prepare yourself for it. Study it carefully for evidence of spiritual gifts. Remember that these gifts might not obviously relate to a specific profession. Record in your journal the list of gifts that your blessing implies.

2. Devote some time to thinking about your childhood. What games did you play? What toys were your favorites? What activities did you participate in when you had complete freedom in how you spent your time? What are your most fun memories? As you consider these questions, look for patterns and themes. What do your memories tell you about your spiritual gifts? What connections do you see between your childhood activities and your current work (or career plans)? Record your thoughts in your journal.

3. Conduct a Reflected Best Self exercise. Specifically, identify between 10 and 20 people who know you well. Ask them each to share with you two to three memories they have of you when you were at your best. Explain to them that they don't need to elaborate on your character traits—just share brief incidents. You will probably get better results if you give people a deadline for when you need their responses. Once you have received your responses, carefully read through the stories. Look for common themes. Record your thoughts in your journal.

4. Seek an understanding of your spiritual gifts in prayer. Consider devoting an upcoming fast to asking the Lord to reveal the gifts He would like you to use and further develop next. As you record your gifts in all of the previous steps, strive to be as specific as you can be in defining them. Instead of "I am good at helping people," for instance, describe specific ways that you are well-suited to help others.

Endnotes

1. McConkie, B. R. 1985. *A New Witness for the Articles of Faith.* Deseret Book, page 371.
2. Hales, R. D. "Gifts of the Spirit," *Ensign,* February 2002, page 16.
3. Groberg, J. H. 1979. "What is Your Mission." See speeches.byu.edu for devotional delivered May 1, 1979.

Notes

CHAPTER 5

The Calling that Chooses You

CORRECTING HERESY #3:
"YOU GET TO CHOOSE YOUR CALLING IN LIFE"

In 2003, Jacob was a psychology student at a major university, and in need of a summer job. His fiancée had worked as a gardener for the city, so she made a phone call to the Parks Department to inquire about job openings for him. Jacob landed a job as the crew leader of the weed-whacking and lawn edging crew. His supervisor warned him that it would be hot, difficult work, but it would provide Jacob the opportunity to learn how to supervise other people. At first, Jacob felt that the work was beneath him. He was an advanced college student, after all! However, he decided that if he was going to do the job, he should do the best work he could. To this day, he doesn't think the parks have ever been as well-kept as they were that summer.

As his summer work drew to a close, Jacob wondered what job he could find next to help him get through school. One day, his boss called him into the office and told Jacob about a part-time opening in the Power Department as a meter reader. Because Jacob had done so well leading the edging crew, his boss recommended him for the job. He was hired. Jacob's work demands now included walking 6 to 8 miles per day to read meters. Again, he felt that he was overqualified for the work, but decided to be the best meter reader he could be.

Later that year, Jacob graduated from the university with a Bachelor's degree in psychology. But job prospects were discouraging. "What in the world am I going to do with this degree?," Jacob wondered. He gradually realized that he had no clear idea of what he wanted to do for a career. He had thought his degree would lead him naturally to a desirable job, but he had given surprisingly little thought to exactly what kind of work he would most like to do.

While Jacob was agonizing about his future, a full-time position in the drafting/engineering side of the Power Department became available. Jacob had never imagined working full-time for the city. He had always had "bigger" plans for himself, which he now had to admit were actually not concrete plans at all. But he had few other options. So, he interviewed for the position, got the job, and started a couple of weeks later.

To his surprise, Jacob found that he enjoyed his new job. He started learning new skills and technologies, excelled at them, and soon became known as the "graphic design guru" of the city. Once again, he had misgivings about whether this was really the work he should be doing, but he tried to learn as much and do as well as he could.

After a year in that position, another job opening—a managerial position—arose within the Power Department. Given Jacob's limited work experience, it seemed like a long shot. But his college degree paid off, and helped land him the job. Jacob has been in the position for the past seven years now, has thoroughly enjoyed it, and just finished a master's degree in public administration on the side to prepare himself for future promotions. Looking back on how his career has unfolded, Jacob recently shared an epiphany: "Maybe I'm supposed to be exactly where I am. Everything seems to have fallen into place for me to be where I am today."

As a high school student, Jacob never would have listed "Director of a Municipal Power Department" as his dream job. But that's exactly what he is aiming to become now. He's very happy with his work. It makes excellent use of his talents, and it provides a service to the community that Jacob cares about. He didn't set out to make this job his calling in life. But his calling seems to have chosen him.

The Path to Calling Is Not a Straight Line

Heresy #3 is the belief that your calling in life is something you choose. That doesn't seem so heretical on the surface. Latter-day saints are taught from childhood that we are agents who act for ourselves. And we have already seen how the Lord invites His children to pursue good causes "of their own free will" (D&C 58:27). But there is a major difference between choosing the *next step* on your path and choosing the *long-term direction* of the path. The Lord gives you great freedom in choosing what you do next, but he rarely gives you clarity about the twists and turns He has planned for you down the road. He sees the whole journey whereas you often can't see past the next bend in the path.

The third heresy tries to deceive you about the personal control you ought to have over your long-term occupational path. It teaches that you are sole master of your own fate. But in doing so, it fails to account for the guidance of the true Master of your soul, and His ability to intervene in guiding your life.

This heresy could seriously damage your faith and self-esteem. If callings are a matter of your own control, then what does it mean if you encounter a setback? It might mean that you failed! Getting fired becomes a senseless personal tragedy, rather than a God-given test. Missing out on a desired opportunity becomes a personal failing rather than, perhaps, a blessed invitation to redirect your life.

Students of the scriptures should not be at all surprised that the

Lord's followers don't usually get to choose the exact path of their lives. As we mentioned in Chapter 1, the children of Israel spent 40 years wandering aimlessly in the wilderness as they waited to inherit the land they had been promised. They might have gotten there sooner had they been more obedient, but they also would have missed out on valuable training and seasoning that provided the entire nation, and generations to come, a strong sense of identity and the fortitude to withstand future adversity.

Few scriptural stories teach this principle more powerfully than that of Joseph of Egypt. Joseph was a young man of remarkable talents, not the least of which was his spiritual gift for interpreting dreams. As far as we can tell, his only youthful career aspirations were to herd sheep and serve his family. There is no evidence that young Joseph had political aspirations or thought that his interpretive talents would be of professional benefit. But then life started to happen to him.

Joseph's first "job" was that of slave, after his brothers sold him to a nomadic band of Ishmeelites. Landing in Potiphar's household, he honed his managerial acumen, and started to climb a professional ladder. Potiphar "made him overseer over his house, and all that he had he put into his hand" (Genesis 39:4). Just when his "career" seemed to be going in a great direction, Joseph was innocently entrapped by Potiphar's wife in a scandal that cost him not only his job, but his very freedom. Prison certainly seemed like a professional dead-end. But Joseph, undaunted, again rendered service to those in power, ultimately gaining their trust and again rising to a managerial role. The prison keeper "committed to Joseph's hand all the prisoners that were in the prison; and whatsoever they did there, he was the doer of it" (Genesis 39:22).

Joseph couldn't have known that prison, of all places, would give him the best possible opportunity to launch into a glorious career. While there, he became acquainted with Pharoah's chief butler, who, it turns out, desperately needed Joseph's gift for dream interpretation.

Through this connection, Joseph came to the attention of Pharoah himself.

(Now, there is "networking" at its finest! Obviously, the Lord was managing the social circuitry.)

Joseph rose to incredible heights of power and influence working for Pharoah. He led the nation safely through famine, and sired a choice branch of the tribes of Israel.

You are not likely to face as many, or such extreme, career reversals as Joseph did. But you can certainly learn from his responses. He made the best of every setback, trusting in the Lord and seeking to serve in whatever way he could. The Lord was able to shape and use Joseph *because of* his reaction to adversity. Joseph did not deserve to be banished, enslaved, accused, and imprisoned. But had he not weathered those storms, he never would have reached his stunning professional apex.

A more modern example comes from the personal history of Elder Hugh B. Brown. Elder Brown was a field officer in the British Canadian Army, and had worked for ten years to achieve his goal of becoming a general. He had the seniority, the performance record, and had completed all of the necessary examinations. But he was denied his well-deserved promotion because of his religion. He was devastated, bitter, even angry with God. As he wrestled with the seeming injustice, he was reminded of a time when he had aggressively pruned back a bush in his garden so that it would grow better. And he came to understand that God is the gardener of our lives, a Gardener who must sometimes "cut you back" so that you can truly grow. He gave the following counsel to those who wonder why their professional hopes and aspirations sometimes seem thwarted:

> *"You sometimes wonder whether the Lord really knows what he ought to do with you. You sometimes wonder if you know better than he does about what you ought to do and ought to become. ...*

I just want you to know that if you don't get what you think you ought to get, remember, 'God is the gardener here. He knows what he wants you to be.' Submit yourselves to his will. Be worthy of his blessings, and you will get his blessings"[1]

So, if you occasionally feel lost in a professional wilderness, does it mean that the Lord has forgotten you, or loves you less than you thought? On the contrary, the Lord uses winding paths to prepare, instruct and bless you. Your ultimate calling in life may not be a matter of your own choosing. And feeling lost does not mean that there is no professional "promised land" in store for you.

This discussion reminds us of a diagram that made the rounds on social media:

Success   **Success**

what people think   what it really
it looks like   looks like

It's brilliant! We haven't been able to identify the original source. But whoever sketched it understands that people tend to grossly over-simplify the paths of others' success. You might picture Thomas Edison deciding to invent the light bulb and—*voila*—there it is. But that overlooks the fact that Edison labored through countless false starts before he developed a workable technology. When asked about his many "failures" on the way to success, he reportedly quipped, "I have not failed. I've just found 10,000 ways that won't work."

Happily, it probably won't take you 10,000 failures before you find success in your work. But you are fooling yourself if you think you can entirely avoid false starts, reversals, and rocky paths. When you hit those jarring bumps in the road, you may be too quick to despair, or to assume that you are in the wrong place, when actually you are just doing the important work of figuring out the "ways that won't work."

One of our executive students expressed a sense of despair recently. She is well into her career, and recently made a big change to a new job. She truly loves the organization she works for, and her job gives her plenty of developmental challenges. But her supervisor is a poor leader, and she finds herself trying to hold together a fragmented and dysfunctional department full of apathetic colleagues and petty turf wars. She tries valiantly to influence the culture, but faces an uphill battle since her position doesn't give her the authority to call the shots.

As she talked about her workplace, her face assumed a mystified expression. She said something like, "I just don't know how I got here. And I have no idea where to go next. I feel completely lost right now."

Her bafflement rings a bell. We have all felt lost at times. Being lost can bring a wretched, hopeless fear, perhaps not too far removed from the consternation the children of Israel felt as they meandered through a desolate wilderness.

It's a fear that also turns out to be completely unfounded.

The diagram we shared with you earlier inspired Jeff to come up with one of his own. He describes the experiment as follows:

I wanted to try to depict my own career path. The first image represents how I saw my occupational journey by about age 30. At this point in my life, I had changed college majors several times, had worked in a job that I hated, had experienced multiple unexpected reversals during my PhD studies, and was working in an academic position that I enjoyed, but in which I felt unsettled.

My career looks pretty random and meandering at this point. No wonder I often felt adrift.

Let's fast-forward to where I see my career now. Today, I am in my second academic job. The circumstances that led me to my current position were extremely circuitous and unexpected, sometimes even painful. But I have also gradually discovered things I care about very deeply, including a focus in my teaching and research that fits me like a glove. Continuing on from the first diagram, this is how I depict my path now:

There is still a lot of meandering going on in this diagram. But you might also notice a pattern. The fluctuations have narrowed over the years. And even though the path is not a straight line, you can definitely begin to discern an overall direction. In fact, in hindsight, there even seem to be some boundaries that delimit the randomness. When I superimpose them on the diagram, it looks something like this:

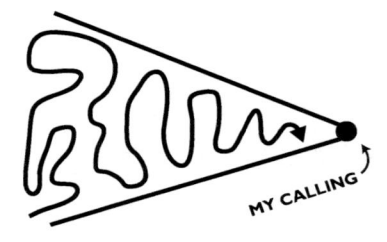

With the benefit of hindsight, all of those seemingly senseless twists and turns now represent a clear pattern. Ten years ago, the pattern was impossible to see, and things really did feel almost random. But today, I have no reason to regret a single fluctuation. Some of the reversals were painful, but they were all essential to the process of zeroing in on my calling in life.

Please note that I drew the diagram to indicate that I have not yet arrived at my precise calling. My career (and life) experiences will still surprise me now and then, and the path will continue to oscillate. But I know now that each turn of the road will help me come to an ever-sharper understanding of my true gifts and passions. The journey will take longer than my mortal span.

Did I Choose the Wrong Path?

You have probably experienced that horrible moment when you realize you have been driving your car in the wrong direction for a long time—maybe hours. Being on the wrong road invariably makes you think about missed opportunities. If you hadn't missed the freeway exit two hours ago, you might have had four more hours of family time at the reunion.

Freeways, though, have the wonderful quality of being vastly interconnected and retraceable. If you lose your way on a road trip, there is always a way back, even if we incur a major delay. But life's highways don't always seem like that. Like Robert Frost notes in his great poem

"The Road Not Taken," when you choose one path over another, you may never be able to go back to the unchosen path.

> *"... Yet knowing how way leads on to way*
> *I doubted if I should ever come back."*[2]

Of course, many life choices are indeed irreversible. If you choose to go to law school instead of medical school, for instance, then most likely you have closed the door on becoming a doctor. So, if you are the kind of person who likes having options, then making big choices can be excruciating—because each choice also seems to represent a forever-lost possibility.

When you buy into the world's dogma that callings are simply a matter of personal choice, this puts tremendous pressure on you, the chooser. You may start to view life as a high-stakes guessing game. If things go badly on your path, you might conclude that you chose the wrong one. What if there is no way back to the right path? Have you forever missed your shot at a fulfilled life?

If you stop and reflect on some of the basic things we know about God and His plan, you can easily see the folly in that kind of thinking. The Savior's Atonement—the very central feature of God's plan—is all about second chances. Father in Heaven provided a Savior precisely to help you when you stumble off His path. It is a bit ironic that people who believe in God's mercy to the repentant sinner can somehow also believe that He would shut the door on your happiness and professional growth just because you made a professional misstep along the way. If God offers second chances to those who wander from His gospel path, why would he deny second chances if you meander on your professional paths? That would be inconsistent with Heavenly Father's compassion toward us.

The choices you make do, of course, have a way of opening some paths and closing off others. But the modern career landscape is an extremely diverse and fluid one. Career changes are common. There are almost always opportunities to shift course, even if it requires sacrifices or further education. More to the point, you can have faith that your Heavenly Father will provide you professional opportunities you might never have anticipated.

Dead-Ends in the Path

The third heresy also has a way of making you feel like a victim. If you believe that you can choose your calling, how do you explain setbacks and road closures on your path? It might feel like someone has cruelly denied you your *right* to a calling. To explore how the third heresy can impact you in the face of disappointment, we would like to introduce you to a young man we will call Grant.

Grant had a very clear vision of his future calling in life. He had done everything he could to make it a reality. But, as he describes below, circumstances tragically took the choice out of his hands:

> *"I have found something which speaks to my soul. I have wanted to be an officer in the United States Marine Corps for a very long time... Despite years of diligent physical preparation, excellent grades, a record of achievement and compelling letters of recommendation from professors and former employers, I have been medically disqualified from service. This has been a terrible blow. I am pursuing waivers in order to protect my ambitions, but I have to face reality—chances are slim to none (worse, probably) that my efforts will come to anything.*
>
> *Given that career paths associated with my college degree are totally unappealing to me, how should I go about finding a new calling in life? Frankly, nothing is nearly as compelling to me as military service."*

Grant's question demanded a careful answer, so Jeff arranged to meet with him. He found Grant to be bright, extremely earnest, and passionate about honoring the men and women who serve in the military. As he talked about his shattered dreams, Grant's heartbreak was palpable. It reminded us of the heartbreak we have seen in other people who have lost their chance at pursuing a chosen calling, such as the person who found he lacked the talent to pursue a career in music, or the aspiring entrepreneur who foregoes her dream venture to care for an ailing spouse.

We wish we had a golden answer for Grant and others who face dashed professional dreams. We don't. But we do know that the third heresy only makes things worse. Jeff's conversation with Grant might offer some insight into how the heresy of chosen callings was inhibiting Grant's thinking. Here is Jeff's recollection of that conversation:

> *I first asked Grant some pointed questions: What sparked his interest in being a Marine officer? What, exactly, did he envision himself doing? Why is it so important to him?*
>
> *Grant explained that being a Marine officer would provide him the perfect blend of at least three of his deepest professional yearnings: physical challenge, mentorship opportunities, and protecting the well-being of servicemen and women. I thought, "He's right. Marine Officer does seem the perfect job for him."*
>
> *But then I explained to Grant an important truth: A calling is not just a job title. Echoing Martin Luther, I explained that a calling is using your gifts to serve others within whatever circumstances God has placed you.*

Notice how this classic definition of calling turns the third heresy on its head. Modern management gurus have urged people to make bold choices to follow their passions in life. The idea is that you decide what you really want to do in life, and then you go out and "sell" the world on why you should be allowed to do it. But the Protestant

The Calling that Chooses You

Reformers taught that a calling means first looking at the situation life has placed you in. Rather than asking "what do *I* really want to do?," you instead look at what people around you need most, and then you identify which of your gifts you can use to serve those needs in your own unique way. In other words, the worlds' version of calling emphasizes self-expression, but the classic version emphasizes service. Both of these are good things. But it doesn't take much reflection about the Savior's teachings to determine which value—self-expression or service—He emphasizes the most.

The classic view of calling is not terribly romantic. It doesn't depict you as a rugged individualist who can chart your own course in life, regardless of what the world gives you. And indeed, it is very worthwhile to celebrate heroic people who blaze new trails because of their single-minded convictions. But for every Christopher Columbus, there are many more "visionaries" who end up falling into obscurity because their personal crusade didn't fit with the needs of the day. The classic view of calling—using your gifts to meet the needs that present themselves to you—is much more realistic, and even liberating. Emphasizing service as the starting point makes callings accessible to virtually everyone. And, as we will argue later, that is a much surer route to fulfillment than putting passion first.

What is Grant to do, though? Despite hearing tidy answers from an egghead professor, he is still feeling the sharp sting of his bitter disappointment.

Jeff encouraged Grant to continue looking for ways around his medical disqualification. Persistence often pays off. But he also encouraged Grant to open his mind to the possibility of letting go of his narrow view of how he can best serve the world. Could it be that the closing of this door was actually an invitation for Grant to walk through a better one? Might Heavenly Father have a different use for Grant's gifts that will bring him even greater joy than military service?

Grant started asking himself the following types of questions: Where else would my combination of gifts lead me? Might I find opportunities to lead and serve my country by working for the government, perhaps in emergency management or disaster relief? Asking these types of questions gradually helped Grant to see that his calling was not limited to a single life path. Grant's unique set of gifts, like your own set, is vitally needed in more than one place. This is why your pursuit of a calling might usher you through a variety of roles during your lifetime.

Incidentally, after further exploration and lots of prayer and fasting, Grant began to pursue a career in health care administration, with a focus on ensuring excellent care for military veterans. He is feeling hope and excitement again. The heartbreaking obstacle of military disqualification helped him find a new way to use his spiritual gifts to serve others.

How Can I Find My Calling When I'm Stuck in this Lousy Job?

We don't want to go too far in dismissing the third heresy, however. Children of God *are* agents who are commanded to "act for themselves and not to be acted upon" (2 Nephi 2:26). You have the power to make a change if you are unhappy with your occupational circumstances.

At some time in your life, you will probably feel "stuck" in circumstances that don't allow you to fully express your gifts. Jeff, for instance, felt stuck in a corporate job that left him feeling numb and alienated. He recalls: "Probably like most people, I handled it badly. I turned inward, I watched the clock, I did enough good work to get by. And I waited every day, hoping for the 'right job' to come along and save me."

Can you see the flaw in Jeff's strategy? By turning his heart off while waiting for career nirvana to arrive, he was actually trapping himself. He had assumed the Rapunzel position: waiting passively in his "prison" for rescue to arrive. If the fairy tale script holds, then the dream job should come galloping on the scene to whisk him away.

Allow us to introduce some harsh reality here.

Most people never find a "dream" job.

Most people struggle away in imperfect, politicized workplaces (home included), wrestling with unsavory or impossible tasks, frequently underused or under-appreciated, and sometimes baffled about the point of it all.

But, as we suggested to Grant, a *job* is not a calling. You will likely never find a single role that will align perfectly with your gifts and talents. There will be aspects of every role that chafe against your uniqueness or feel unnatural to you (motherhood and fatherhood included). There will be expectations that violate your personal priorities. There will be people you are required to serve and partner with who treat you in less than Christ-like ways. At the risk of sounding horribly pessimistic, every job in the world is a little bit lousy. Remember the thorns and thistles that awaited Adam outside the Garden of Eden?

When you let go of the belief that there is some perfect job out there that will reveal your calling to you, you then have to face some tough questions about your own responsibility for finding fulfillment. Once Rapunzel realizes there is no handsome prince on the way, then she has to decide what to do for herself.

So what should Jeff have done in his crummy corporate job instead of biding his time, waiting for happiness to appear? Here's a different script he might have played in his head: "OK. I don't really like this place or the work I've been asked to do. It doesn't *naturally* bring out the best in me. But I wonder what I could start doing that might make this a better place for other people? Is there something creative I can contribute? Can I make things easier, better, more interesting, more fulfilling for my coworkers? Can I surprise and delight my clients?" Unfortunately, these questions never crossed Jeff's mind at the time. He reflects: "I wish now that I had stopped thinking so much about myself and instead asked, 'how can I *serve?*'"

This brings us back to one of the greatest principles we have learned about callings: you discover them while in service to others, rather than in service to self. It's the classic paradoxical principle that Jesus taught: "He that findeth his life shall lose it: and he that loseth his life for my sake shall find it" (Matthew 10:39). Taking the Savior's teachings to heart, and applying them to your career, it becomes clear that "lousy" isn't really about what happens to you at work. Jobs are lousy when you aren't serving anyone.

Let's take the example of a hospital orderly—a person who cleans up bodily fluids and sanitizes the aftermath of disease and death. Can you imagine anything quite so unsavory? The circumstances of such work seem lousy indeed. But research on so-called "dirty work" suggests that hospital orderlies often develop a sense of deep meaning in their work (some even consider it a calling) because of the service it provides to others.[3] Like the zookeepers in our own research, people will willingly—even cheerfully—work in the worst of circumstances if they know they are serving a cause they care about.

But let's put bad jobs into perspective. Having a lousy job is actually not the worst thing that could ever happen to you. A bad job may be painful drudgery, but it's also an opportunity to be refined and *de*fined; bad jobs help you figure out who you are and who you aren't. They also provide an opportunity, as Joseph of Egypt demonstrated, to find creative ways to use your gifts to make the best of a bad situation.

A few of our colleagues—Justin Berg and Adam Grant at Wharton and Victoria Johnson at the University of Michigan –recently published a study about how people cope with "missed callings." They studied teachers who feel that they were meant to be something else, and who feel unfulfilled in their teaching jobs. The research found that some people coped by pursuing their passions as a hobby outside of work.

Others, however, found creative ways to bring their unique gifts (i.e., their missed callings) *into the classroom* as part of their unique teaching style. For instance, one teacher who felt called to be a musician started bringing his guitar to school and found ways to use his musical gifts to enhance his instruction. Using spiritual gifts to season their work didn't entirely resolve the teachers' sense that they were off the path. However, teachers who brought their passions with them to the classroom reported more satisfaction and a greater sense of contribution.

Is it possible that when you complain about having a lousy job, you are simply voicing a lame excuse not to be creative? Granted, there are some pretty boring, lonely, and stale jobs out there. But can't you still find innovative ways to use your spiritual gifts, even in the worst jobs? Some new research on a technique called "job crafting" suggests you can.

Crafting Your Job

If you have a job, you probably also have a list of things you have to do: formal job expectations. Most of them are non-negotiable, right? They are the things you absolutely have to get done. But you might have more discretion than you realize when it comes to *how* you do things.

Let's take accountants as an example. You probably know the old stereotype: accountants are unimaginative pencil-pushers who are slaves to the rigid rules that govern their work. But the reality is, of course, much more nuanced. Far from being a homogenous herd of mindless, conventional bookkeepers, accountants cover the gamut of personality traits—introverts and extraverts, liberals and conservatives, artists and technicians. Must they all mask these unique traits to become the conventional accountant? Of course not. There are a million different kinds of accountants, each bringing their own talents to work. Some accountants are the kind that can explain complex transactions with flair and energy. Others have a gift for helping clients see the long-term implications of their financial decisions. Still others have a gift for graphic design; they can create tables and charts that both wow and educate their clients.

This principle is true of any job, including homemaking. Even on an assembly line, there are opportunities to put your own unique stamp on the work you do. A job is much more than a static to-do list. Instead, try thinking of your job as a box full of building blocks that you can arrange and combine in many different ways. This is what our aforementioned colleague, Justin Berg, this time with coauthors Jane Dutton of the University of Michigan and Amy Wrzesniewski of Yale University, have called "job crafting." Their research shows that people can improve their jobs from the inside out by crafting what they do so that their work aligns better with their talents and interests. You can craft a job in at least three different ways:

1. Change what you do, or how you do it. (For example, you might negotiate with your supervisor to focus on tasks that better reflect your gifts, or you might invent a new method to do them.)
2. Change how you interact with other people at work. (For example, you might offer to train other people.)
3. Change how you define the work you do. (For example, you might think about the people your work helps rather than defining your work by the menial tasks you do.)[4]

Whichever of these techniques you use, Berg and his colleagues have shown that crafting your job will increase your satisfaction. That means that if you feel alienated by your job, or mired in drudgery, you don't have to postpone finding your calling. You can start now, even in a lousy job, to build your gifts into the work you are currently doing.

Something sort of magical happens to people who make the most of their jobs—even the crummy ones. They tend to get noticed. In fact, the surest way to *get beyond* your lousy job is by throwing your heart into it, using your spiritual gifts to help other people in, and around, your organization. Doing so will illuminate your gifts so that people (including yourself) can see what they are. You will become extraordinary in your crummy job. And—here's the clincher—when you become extraordinary, the "right job" is much more likely to find you.

Can You Find Your Calling If You Are Unemployed?

When the economy is bad, the third heresy can give you fits. Remember that the third heresy is a mistaken belief that your calling is a matter of personal choice. Well, when the job market tightens, your choices begin to disappear. There are simply not many jobs to choose from. If you believe life owes you the choice of your dream job, then a poor economy feels like a raw deal. You might start to blame Congress, or Wall Street, or corporate greed for taking away your *right* to have a dream job (or maybe any job at all). Feeling like a victim is a first step to despair. And the third heresy has the seeds of victimhood built right into it.

The cold truth is that you may suffer joblessness during your lifetime. And joblessness is hard on us. Research shows that unemployment can have a devastating long-term personal impact. A recent study tracked people who had spent significant time being unemployed. It found that these people, compared to those who hadn't lost their jobs, made 20% less money as long as 15-20 years after they had been laid off.[5] Other studies show that unemployment strains family relationships, diminishes self-respect, increases the likelihood of depression and other health problems, and even reduces life expectancy.[6] Unemployment makes you feel out of control of your life. It gives you a gnawing, destructive sense of purposelessness. You may start to feel that you have nothing to contribute.

We have observed the battle to maintain dignity during unemployment in Ken, one of our dearest mutual friends. Ken is a highly gifted and truly wonderful person. But somehow his career path has often been rocky, and sometimes even bruising. While raising a family of five, he has had some extended periods of unemployment. He has weathered difficult supervisors, companies that have gone out of business, and being laid off. All of this has provided severe tests of faith, and self-esteem, for Ken and his wife. For those of us who have watched Ken's struggles, it has been baffling to try to understand why someone who is so dynamic, so interpersonally effective, so smart, and so faithful could experience so much employment adversity.

We can't claim to have easy solutions for the adversity of unemployment. But we do believe that a sense of calling can help you get through it with much less despair and self-doubt. The world's doctrine is that you don't have a calling unless you have a job. Not true! Even if you don't have a job, you still have spiritual gifts that are ideally suited to meeting specific needs of the people around you. Recognizing your spiritual gifts is how you inoculate yourself against the buffetings of the job market. If you are unemployed, define yourself by your gifts—not by your lack of a job. And then seek ways to use your gifts so that they stay sharp. Consider donating your spiritual gifts to worthy causes, perhaps through public service or volunteering. If you continue to exercise and hone your calling, the value of your gifts are more likely to become evident to others, and the likelihood increases that people will want to pay you a fair wage for them.

This is what Ken has done. Even as he battled the despair of unemployment, he kept honing his skills. Gifted in graphic design and marketing, he worked to master new areas of interest, including Sales Operations, a relatively new discipline in the business world. He sought opportunities to freelance, and to offer his services (often for free) to people who needed help starting up small businesses. He stayed in touch with his spiritual gifts, and exercised faith. Today, Ken is stably employed in an organization he enjoys and pursues a successful consulting practice on the side. He has also found great satisfaction in teaching courses at a technical college. It turns out that the breadth of experiences he gained in the many organizations he has worked for have prepared him perfectly to educate others. The years of adversity are paying off.

At a minimum, employing your gifts in some useful way is a healthier and far more productive strategy than withdrawing from the world and anxiously waiting by the phone for a job to come to you. When you withdraw, you run the risk that your unused gifts will stagnate (the result of "hiding your light under a bushel"). You also cut yourself off from relationships and experiences that might open unexpected opportunities to you. Notice how the Lord instructs his children when they are traveling through a treacherous wilderness. When the Brother of Jared led his family away toward an unknown promised land, the Lord told him to "go at the head of them down into the valley which is northward. *And there will I meet thee* and I will go before thee" (Ether 1:42; emphasis added). Our heavenly navigator is absolutely reliable, but He usually joins you after you take the initiative to venture out onto the path first. He meets you *on the way.* You can't expect the tender mercies that will open new opportunities if you don't first exercise the faith to extend yourself and engage with the world around you.

Can You Still Find Your Calling if You Choose to Stay at Home?

It's also vital to understand that you can still exercise your calling in life if you *choose* not to be employed. The way the world equates calling with a job does a terrible disservice, for instance, to women who prioritize motherhood over professional careers. The media and other leading voices sometimes express thinly veiled disdain for women who choose to do their life's work on the home front. They imply that women who stay at home are somehow suppressing their potential and succumbing to archaic societal expectations. This disdain, so hostile to the sanctity of the family, is a terrible expression of the third heresy, which suggests that stay-at-home moms are selling themselves short. But if a calling means using your spiritual gifts to serve the people around you, then motherhood and family life become the noblest and most urgent expressions of calling.

Actually, one of our favorite stories about professional callings is that of a stay-at-home mom named Michelle. Motherhood is Michelle's highest priority, and yet she has felt a pull toward keeping her professional skills active. Her story can teach us a lot about how important it is for women to trust the inspiration they receive about their calling in life.

Like many young people, Michelle had a hard time deciding what to study in college, and agonized a lot about what she should be when she grew up. Her memories about that time show that she had fallen squarely into the third heresy trap: "I thought if I didn't find the one right path, I would mess up my life forever!"

It was during this time of uncertainty and stress that Michelle sought a priesthood blessing from her father. Although the blessing provided comfort to her then, it would take years for her to fully appreciate how that blessing would guide her. Among other things, the blessing promised her that God would help her to discern her mission as she went along through life. It also told her that there were *many* ways she could accomplish her mission in life. This diminished her fear of missing her "one right path." In fact, her path soon began to unfold in ways that surprised her.

Michelle served a mission, even though that hadn't been her original plan. She decided to get an MBA, an idea that she said came out of the blue. While in school, she discovered dreams and passions that she hadn't recognized before. One of them was a fascination with technology in management. She landed a job in telecommunications and business process in New Jersey, and loved it.

She also met her husband in New Jersey, and quit her job to raise her children. Over time, she found ways to keep her resumé and her network current even as a stay-at-home mom. She did some consulting work on the side and tried her hand at starting a business. She became a member of the undergraduate advisory board of the Marriott School of Management at BYU. She anticipated going back into the corporate world at some point.

But that dream began to feel impossible when Michelle developed serious health problems that severely limited her energy and mobility. For someone who had been a "doer" all her life, this was a monumental challenge. Not only did her illness threaten Michelle's ability to return someday to the work she loved, it also made motherhood—her most important job—more difficult than ever. But Michelle remained inspired by her father's blessing. The Lord had promised that He would guide her to find her mission in life. She still had a driving desire to use her talents to serve in the world around her.

Michelle discovered that one of the few things she had enough energy and time for was blogging. Writing a blog also fit well with Michelle's gifts for technology and communications. She envisioned a blog that would work as a missionary tool by introducing others to the lives and beliefs of LDS women (see MormonWoman.org). Michelle didn't anticipate how large the response to her blog would be, nor the new connections, interests, and directions it would foster for her. For instance, driven by the searches on her site, and inspired by Elder Ballard's 2010 General Conference talk on addiction, she became deeply involved in helping organizations and individuals access more online information about addiction and recovery.

Looking back, Michelle can see the hand of the Lord in almost every step that led her to the blog. She realizes that without her health challenges, she never would have seen this opportunity. She reflects:

"I couldn't have planned it. I couldn't have set a goal that said 'I'm going to be *this* when I grow up.' I'm along for the ride. It's very different from having a dream and pursuing it with all your might. It's trying to keep an eye open for doors, and having my limitations be part of what opened those doors."

As a blog writer, Michelle didn't have a job in the traditional sense, but she did relish a sense of calling, even as she struggled to balance her professional gifts with her family responsibilities. She says:

"First and foremost, I want to validate motherhood. But our culture is swinging the other direction. It's almost minimizing motherhood as a career. The more we validate motherhood, the less conflict mothers feel. Women don't have to do something else to prove their worth or fulfill expectations.

"We should cherish motherhood because there is nothing more important. But God gives us gifts and talents to use them. It's just a matter of discerning how to go about it. He expects me to always be asking if I'm doing this in the right balance.

"We worship a God of abundance and compensatory blessings. He is not out to strip us of what matters to us, even though he asks for sacrifice. In reality, I figured out more of who I am because I'm a mom, and that gives me the ability to be more fulfilled in other parts of my life."

Michelle's path toward her calling was less than clear. Eventually, she felt a strong prompting to pull back from some of her volunteer involvement. Was the Lord signaling to her that she was entering a season when her family needed her undivided attention? Did He have new unanticipated opportunities and challenges in store for her? Despite a lack of clear answers, Michelle learned to trust the promptings that guide her calling. As she put it, "I want to be potter's clay."

If, as we have argued, callings are about finding that place where your unique gifts and talents can be used to benefit others, then motherhood is as eligible for the status of calling as any professional identity. In fact President Harold B. Lee stated: "The most important of the Lord's work that you will ever do will be the work you do within the walls of your own home"[7] Do you have to be formally employed in order to fulfill your calling in life? Clearly not.

Postscript:

A year after our interview with Michelle, she received a phone call out of the blue requesting that she meet with a nonprofit organization about an online community she had created. She was offered a job that week, and felt inspired to take it. This position eventually opened up an opportunity for her to collaborate with others on the creation of a new nonprofit organization focused on raising children in a digital world. Michelle is its Executive Director, a part-time role she has found to be more conducive to her family responsibilities than she would have imagined. Looking back, Michelle can see that her health challenges actually opened the door to this opportunity; her current job is a direct result of the online work that her illness propelled her toward. She told us, "My work brings together so many of my interests, gifts, and passions that sometimes it takes my breath away... This opportunity has let me know that God cares about me. He is aware of me. He is weaving all the pieces of my life together—and always has been—in ways that I could never have dreamed."

Indeed, the Lord always promises to magnify our gifts if we seek to use them in service. Stay-at-home moms can exercise their calling in life whether or not the Lord leads them into professional involvement.

Calling and Control

Why is the third heresy such a popular one? Part of the reason is that we human beings crave a sense of control. We like to chart our course and then follow our path to a chosen destination. Taking accountability for our own actions, setting and achieving goals, choosing good causes to pursue—all of these things are consistent with the Lord's teachings about agency and His commandment to His children to "act for themselves and not be acted upon" (2 Nephi 2:26).

But lest we take these teachings to an extreme the Lord does not intend, we also need to balance the gospel truths that we are dependent on the Lord for everything we have (see Mosiah 4:19), that He leads us in ways we can't always anticipate (see 2 Nephi 10:20), and that He is the One who provides the means for us to "sojourn in the wilderness" (1 Nephi 17:3). The third heresy—that your calling is simply a matter of personal choice—is not so much an out-and-out lie, but rather a distortion of the doctrine of agency that leaves out the blessed influence Heavenly Father has in shaping the path to your calling in life.

What To Do Now

If you are currently unemployed:

1. In your journal, generate a list of possible volunteer activities you might pursue that use the spiritual gifts you already realize you have (perhaps the ones that you identified in the last chapter). Think about both community and church-related service. Even if it's not clear to you yet how you would go about rendering a particular type of service, include it on your list.

2. Add to the list some other volunteer activities that appeal to

you, but that don't clearly relate to spiritual gifts you already have.

3. Go through your list and evaluate which of these activities has the greatest likelihood of stretching you and honing your gifts. Also, evaluate which of the activities are the likeliest to connect you with people who might recognize the financial value of your spiritual gifts.

4. Prayerfully choose one activity that you will actually pursue. Begin today by calling organizations and community or church leaders that might be able to direct you to ways to pursue the service. As you engage in service, record what you are learning about your gifts.

5. Make a list of people who would particularly appreciate or benefit from your spiritual gifts. Develop a plan to improve your professional network by reaching out to at least one of these people. As you contact them, make some offer to serve them (rather than asking for a favor).

If you are currently underemployed (or in a job that doesn't make use of your spiritual gifts):

1. In your journal, make a list of things about your work place or organization that need improvement. Spend enough time to develop a thorough list of ideas.

2. Review the list and consider which of these issues you feel best equipped to make a difference with (in other words, which of these problems could benefit most from the spiritual gifts that you identified in the last chapter).

3. Prayerfully identify at least one area where you will take initiative to address a problem at work.

4. Prayerfully identify at least one person in your organization who is in a position of influence and who is likely to support

your efforts to address the problem you have chosen. Meet individually with the people (or person) you identified and describe your plan, asking for support. Take their counsel to heart as they advise you how (and whether) to proceed. If they counsel you not to proceed, investigate with them other ways that you might use your gifts to benefit the organization. Think carefully about whose support you need for your initiative, and how to proceed in a way that will be politically acceptable.

5. Begin as soon as possible to implement the plans you have agreed to.

6. As you pursue your initiative, record what you are learning about your spiritual gifts. Consider ways that you can use what you have learned to find a better position in your organization, or to offer your talents to other organizations.

7. Make a list of people who would particularly appreciate or benefit from your spiritual gifts. Develop a plan to improve your professional network by reaching out to at least one of these people. As you contact this person, make some offer to use your spiritual gifts to benefit him or her (rather than asking for a favor).

If you are happily employed:

1. In your journal, write an entry that begins with the phrase, "If I found myself suddenly unemployed, I would do the following:…" In your entry, explore ways that you could continue to use your professional skills even if you weren't employed (e.g., by rendering service to others).

2. Carefully evaluate how well-equipped you would be for unemployment at this point in your life. List steps that you should take, in each of the following categories, to prepare yourself to

weather extended unemployment: Financial, Spiritual, Social, and Professional.

3. Reviewing the list of steps you have generated, prayerfully identify one initiative you will take to prepare yourself to maintain a sense of calling even if you were to lose your employment. Begin right away to implement the plan.

4. Make a list of people who would particularly appreciate or benefit from your spiritual gifts that you identified in the last chapter. Develop a plan to improve your professional network by reaching out to one or more of these people. As you contact them, make some offer to serve them (rather than asking for a favor).

Endnotes

1. Brown, H. B. 1973. The Currant Bush. *New Era,* January.
2. Frost, R. 1920. *Mountain Interval.* New York: Henry Holt and Company.
3. Reed, D. A. 1989. An orderly world: the social construction of reality within an occupation. Unpublished doctoral dissertation. Bloomington: Indiana University.
4. Berg, J. M., Dutton, J. E, & Wrzesnieski, A. 2008. What is Job Crafting and Why Does it Matter? Center for Positive Organizational Scholarship. University of Michigan.
5. von Wachter, T., Song, J. & Manchester, J. 2009, *Long-Term Earnings Losses Due to Mass Layoffs During the 1982 Recession: An Analysis Using U.S. Administrative Data from 1974 to 2004.* (unpublished; New York: Columbia University).
6. Appelbaum, B. 2012. The Enduring Consequences of Unemployment. *The New York Times,* March 28.
7. Lee, H. B. 1973. *Strengthening the Home,* page 7.

Notes

CHAPTER 6

Families and Callings

**CORRECTING HERESY #4:
"YOU HAVE TO SET ASIDE YOUR CALLING
IN ORDER TO SUPPORT OUR FAMILY"**

To most people, Brandon's job sounds very exotic—even exciting. He works on a large consulting contract with an Arabic ministry, providing strategic guidance to an agency workforce of 30,000 plus employees. The job has given his family the opportunity to live in the Middle East, to meet fascinating people, and to render important service in the church. But any bloom of excitement that Brandon feels about his work has faded.

When Brandon was 18, he received his patriarchal blessing. The blessing put great emphasis on his occupational choices. It instructed him to choose an occupation in which he would be the "servant of all and not the servant of a few," and told him that he should use his work to help many people who could not help themselves. To equip himself to render this kind of service, Brandon and his family felt impressed to make some heavy sacrifices so that he could earn not one, but two master's degrees.

Brandon felt closely guided by the spirit in making these decisions, but after completing his education, his family was burdened with so much student debt that he felt he needed to make salary the top consideration in choosing a career. Prioritizing his financial stewardship toward his family is what led Brandon to his current work, and he is grateful to have the means to support his family. However, as he thinks about the work he is doing, he feels that it falls short of the instructions in his patriarchal blessing.

As he soldiers through his consulting job, Brandon continually feels a yearning to teach. The happiest time in his career was a brief stint when he taught a university class. He has strongly considered earning a PhD, but he feels it might be selfish of him to take off more time for school and make his family go through even more financial sacrifices.

Meanwhile, Brandon finds that he usually can't spark the same sort of energy in his consulting clients as he did in his students. This frustrates him. He doesn't see how his work is making a difference. However, despite his dissatisfaction, Brandon has received repeated spiritual confirmations that he is where he is supposed to be right now.

He expressed the following thoughts about his career:

"I read about others finding passion in their work. And my situation has usually been far from that. I do my work well, I get promoted, my performance evaluations are uniformly high. And yet, work is what I do to take care of my family. There have been many times I have had a passion for work, but almost always it's been sapped and drained away by organizational politics or inertia... Blessedly, I have surrendered hope for great fulfillment in my career."

There is something tragic in Brandon's final statement. Is it ever a "blessed" event when you "surrender hope?" The resignation to meaningless work that Brandon describes here is a very common manifestation of another worldly heresy about work. And this heresy seems particularly common among people of faith, especially those who, like Latter-day Saints, place a high premium on family stewardship.

The fourth heresy is "you should set aside your calling in life in order to support your family." This is a tricky heresy to talk about, because "family first" is an unequivocally true principle. And parents do indeed have a divinely mandated responsibility to provide for their children. "The Family: A Proclamation to the World" states that parents "will be held accountable before God" for their obligation to care for the physical needs of their children, and it gives fathers a special charge to "provide the necessities of life and protection for their families."

So who are we to criticize someone who has given up on career fulfillment for the sake of family? To be crystal clear, by no means do we wish to condemn devoted parents who have put financial stability ahead of personal passions and dreams. But we want to challenge a false dichotomy here: the perceived either/or choice between meaningful work and family duty. In this chapter, we will show that the fourth heresy reflects a misunderstanding of the nature of callings. In fact, abandoning hope of finding your calling may do a disservice to your family.

Sacrificing for Family

Sacrificing for future generations is one of the most inspiring traits of humankind. In the Church, we cherish our pioneer legacy because of our gratitude to those who gave up comforts and safety so that we can enjoy a flourishing Church and comfortable life today. Most of us benefit directly from parents, grandparents, and other ancestors who did hard things so that our lives would be easier. The willingness we humans have to give of ourselves for future generations is a marvelous testament to the spirit of Elijah, which "shall turn the heart of the fathers to the children" (Malachi 4:6).

Because caring for our families is our most important responsibility, we have a duty to set aside personal desires for the good of spouse and children. As a result, many people, like Brandon, feel compelled to choose a job that makes as much money as possible to ensure the family's security, even if they dislike the work that they do. And there *is* nobility in this sort of sacrifice. You may have been moved by stories of fathers and mothers who spend countless hours of drudgery to provide their children opportunities for education and other blessings. We do not wish to subtract one iota from the sacred offering of parents who give up personal gratification to bless their children.

But we are concerned—deeply so—about people of faith surrendering to the idea that their family responsibilities require them to give up their calling in life forever. When you regretfully abandon your spiritual gifts, you are succumbing to the sort of defeatist resignation that the adversary uses to discourage us. How long can you grind away at hopelessly meaningless work without eventually coming to resent it? Perhaps you might even begin to resent the family obligations that you believe are keeping you chained to a miserable work life?

How Meaningless Work Impacts Your Family

One danger of doing meaningless work to support your family is that it may actually interfere with your ability to be a good spouse and parent. Jeff recalls how he encountered this reality:

I remember how excited I was when I landed my first "real" job after college. The thrill of bringing home a paycheck was liberating. But the exhilaration wore off very quickly when I realized that I couldn't buy into the values of my company. I felt alienated by the company's overwhelming profit motive. I hungered to work for something more than enriching the corporate bottom line. I couldn't see how my work was helping anyone.

At first, I told myself that home would be my refuge from the frustrations of work. I could come home from the daily grind and devote myself to what I really cared about: my wife and new son. As the months wore on, however, I found it increasingly difficult to "turn off" my feelings about work when I got home. I felt depleted by the end of the day, and couldn't muster the energy, or manufacture the cheerfulness that my family deserved. Looking back, I can see now that my gnawing discontent about my job was infecting my family relationships. It's not that I was neglecting my family or acting monstrous to them. Rather, there was just less of me to give to them.

When I contrast that period with my current situation, the difference is astonishing. I still have hard days at work, of course. But today I am doing work that brings out the best in me. I can see how my talents help me to serve. And when I go home, I may be physically tired, but I'm psychologically and spiritually energized. I enjoy telling my children about my work, and I believe they have come to respect what I do.

Jeff's experience illustrates an interesting principle about work/family balance. That is, you can't easily separate the emotions you feel at work with the emotions that you bring home at the end of the day. Researchers have been studying the emotional tensions between work and family for years. Up until the last decade, scholars had fallen into two camps. The "compensation camp" argued that people who are unhappy with their work compensate by pouring their heart into family, and vice-versa. The "spillover camp" argued that people's unhappiness at work infects their happiness at home, and vice-versa. Neither of those views is very encouraging. Both focus on unhappiness.

Recent research, however, has explored a much more encouraging phenomenon, called "work-family enrichment." In a nutshell, it means that when you are engaged in personally meaningful activities, whether at home or at work, other aspects of your life are enriched and increase in meaningfulness. Work-family enrichment is a virtuous cycle that builds a greater sense of balance. This is not to say, of course, that once you have found meaningful work, the challenge of balancing your work and home life goes away. Far from it. But it does mean that if both your work and home life are consistent with your basic values and identity, you can transition much more smoothly between them.

Think of it this way: If you spend your work day acting the part of something you aren't (maybe you have to pretend to be a hard-nosed disciplinarian even though that isn't your nature), then when you get home you not only have to carve out time for family, but you also have to shed a "costume" that you've been wearing all day. It won't come off as easily as you might think.

On the other hand, if your workday allows you to do things you really believe in, then when you walk in the door at home, you are primed and ready to engage with your family in your natural way. There is no awkward transition period as you "put back on" your real self. You may not gain more hours in your day, but it will feel like you have more time because you can "hit the ground running" as you walk in the door. That's the essence of work-family enrichment.

Opportunities for work-family enrichment are important because we humans are just not very well-equipped to turn our emotions on and off at a moment's notice. You might think you are a good actor, and can put on your "game face" for work even if you find it soul-squashing. But you are probably fooling yourself. Even great professional actors talk about how a role they play on stage or film tends to infect the rest of their lives. The great British actor Kenneth Branagh had this to say about the dark, brooding, unhappy character he plays on the PBS television series "Wallander":

> *"I cannot come back to him comfortably. It's never been, 'Oooh, I've got a nice job on the telly.' Every single time it feels like hard work—hard in that I find it difficult. In the early days, I had to do jolly things any chance I could: at the weekend wear bright clothes, go to flower shows. But now I'm better at compartmentalising, being him for the least amount of time I need to be."*[1]

If the best professional actors find it emotionally taxing to inhabit roles that don't fit their natural personalities, why should you think that you can spend 40 or more hours a week playing a part that is not yours to play... and then immediately rebound to your best self when you return home?

Yes, sacrificing your professional happiness in order to provide for your family's financial needs is noble. But the costs may be great. You simply can't put a price on what it means to your children to have a fulfilled, energized parent when you end your day's work. If you are providing for them financially, but feel stunted in providing for them emotionally and spiritually, then it may be better to make less money at a job that helps you be your best self.

Spiritual Dangers of Putting Money First

But it is not just emotional spillover that concerns us. There is also a spiritual dimension of work that Jacob, the Book of Mormon prophet, drives home: "Before ye seek for riches, seek ye for the kingdom of God. And after ye have obtained a hope in Christ ye shall obtain riches, if ye seek them; and ye will seek them for the intent to do good—to clothe the naked, to feed the hungry, and to liberate the captive, and administer relief to the sick and the afflicted" (Jacob 2:18–19).

Clearly, the desire for wealth is not itself a virtuous motive. In fact, the Lord *never* gives scriptural approval for self-gratification as a motive for amassing wealth. At the very most, the only reason He ever gives us for seeking wealth is to bless other people, not ourselves.

As we have talked to young LDS people about their professional motives, we have grown concerned that some of them may misinterpret Jacob's teaching. We fear that some saints stop at the semicolon in verse 19 (in other words, all they hear is "ye shall obtain riches, if you seek them"). They think they hear the Lord saying, "if you are faithful, then the Lord will help you get rich"—almost as if wealth is evidence of the

Lord's approval. But this interpretation is not at all consistent with a careful reading of verse 19.

Why is working for money spiritually dangerous? Here is a sober warning: "But the laborer in Zion shall labor for Zion; for if they labor for money they shall perish." (2 Nephi 26:31). Similarly, Nephi warns us not to spend our labor on "that which cannot satisfy" (2 Nephi 9:51), by which he means material wealth. Over and over again, the scriptures provide examples of wealth-focused people succumbing to pride, vanity, and selfishness. In fact, we have been unable to find a single scriptural example of a people who stayed faithful at the same time they celebrated their wealth.

The soul-destroying nature of materialism is one of the most consistent lessons of the Book of Mormon. Perhaps the Lord emphasizes it so much because we live in a day of previously unimaginable comforts and luxuries. Although you might scoff inwardly at the silly superficiality of materialistic people in the Book of Mormon, you may not always recognize that your own "ornaments" (and cars, and boats, and houses, and toys) are just as distracting as the "tinkling ornaments, and cauls, and round tires like the moon" in ancient time (see 2 Nephi 13:18–23). Even the poorest of those reading this book are probably outrageously wealthy compared to people of ancient scripture (not to mention a large percentage of the citizens of the world today). We cannot afford to ignore scriptural warnings about the dangers of wealth.

But what do these ominous scriptural warnings have to do with your professional choices? If we believe Jacob's teachings, it appears that it's all about your motives. If you have chosen your job purely to make money—and not primarily to serve others—then you may be in dangerous territory.

Some readers might object at this point and say, "Wait a minute, what about people who are desperate just to make ends meet? How can you criticize someone for working for money when they are just trying to survive?" Of course, our intent is not to criticize industrious people who are scraping to get by. We include in this category people in developing economies who have precious few opportunities for developing their gifts. But our point is this: Even the least privileged workers still have a choice about the motives they bring to their work. They can choose to make money their idol—the all-consuming goal. Or they can follow the example of the Saints in Africa as described by Elder John B. Dickson in his April 2013 General Conference talk:

> *"The gospel in Africa is going to a happy people, very unencumbered by the trappings that affect the lives of many in the West. They are not concerned about having endless material possessions.*
>
> *It has been said of Africans that they have very little of that which matters least and a great deal of that which matters most. They have little interest in enormous homes and the finest cars but great interest in knowing their Heavenly Father and His Son, Jesus Christ, and in having eternal families. As a natural result of their faith, the Lord is lifting them in meaningful ways."*

The Savior also had something very pointed to say about financial motives: "No servant can serve two masters: for either he will hate the one, and love the other; or else he will hold to the one, and despise the other. Ye cannot serve God and mammon" (Luke 16:13). Mammon is a horrible master because it is so very demanding. If you measure your success by the attainment of worldly wealth, then you can never really reach satisfaction. There will always be someone wealthier than you are, so the idol of mammon constantly compels you to put in more time and effort to get ahead. These are the seeds of workaholism.

Does a preoccupation with making money distract you from your spiritual life? Your family life? Does it cause you to work longer hours than you ought to? Industriousness is one of those virtues that become a vice when overused. In fact, Alma chapter 4 shows us that industriousness in the pursuit of wealth is a peril to the church in general. The members of the church at that time "began to wax proud" because of the fineries, which "they had obtained *by their industry*" (emphasis added). Eventually, their materialism led to apostasy and destruction. Enthroning money as your primary motive for work is not just a bad idea, it is "the root of all evil" (1 Timothy 6:10).

Making Ends Meet or Pursuing Higher Ends

Stuart had a doctoral student who felt torn between professional dreams and family needs. Rajeev was a bright and well-respected human resources manager in a multinational firm based in India. But he didn't feel complete. He had a passion for helping people to grow and develop, but he felt his work was not giving him the chance to realize that passion. After long deliberation, he decided to pursue a PhD in the United States and launch an academic career. He quit his high-profile job, uprooted his family, and moved to St. Louis to get his degree at Washington University.

Although he was a very good student, Rajeev soon found that the intense pressures of a PhD program, and the distance from home and family, were causing his wife great stress. Other family challenges soon surfaced back home in India, and Rajeev realized that his decision to get a PhD was placing a tremendous burden on his family. He decided to quit the PhD program and return home to help with family issues. He got his old job back, and reconciled himself to a less-than-fulfilling career.

But a few years later, Stuart received an email from Rajeev with an update. Rajeev explained that when he returned to India, he had continued to work in human resource roles in two prominent companies. Eventually, an opportunity arose for him to get training as an executive coach. In this new role, Rajeev designed a two-day workshop for managers in his company to help them discover their strengths at work. His supervisors loved the workshop and Rajeev began delivering it to more seasoned managers throughout the company. His success in this effort led to the creation of a new group within the corporation, called "Capability Development." Rajeev was appointed as leader of this group—and thus found himself directly involved in his passion for helping people develop. He concluded:

"I feel all these years—the HR work, the PhD preparation, and all the reading I did around that time—as well as learnings from my own journey and struggle was a preparation for THIS. IT IS A NEW BEGINNING and I am convinced I was meant to do this work. I feel what one is supposed to feel when you find your 'calling.'"

Rajeev decided to put his family before his professional dreams. But in one of the merciful ironies that often accompany such sacrifices, that very decision is what allowed him to discover his calling.

Let's return to the heresy that launched this chapter: the idea that sometimes you might have to give up on your calling in life in order to support your family financially. That statement might be true if you define calling narrowly as your "dream job." It would indeed be irresponsible for one of us authors to doggedly pursue a career in the NBA while our families starved (which, they no doubt would!). But remember that a calling is not a dream job. A calling means using your divinely appointed gifts to serve Heavenly Father's children—and for most people, there are many ways to do that.

The real problem with the fourth heresy is the false dichotomy it creates. It suggests that you have to choose between using your spiritual gifts and supporting your family. Would a loving Heavenly Father give you spiritual gifts and then ask you to suppress them? He gave them to you precisely because He expects you to use them so that "all may be profited thereby" (DC 46: 12).

When you find yourself in dire financial straits, that is precisely the time that you should be thinking *most* about your calling in life, and about your spiritual gifts—because they are the tools Heavenly Father has given you to do your best work. You might have to take a job that you don't love. The temptation then is to say, "I'm just making ends meet—working for the money and hating every minute of it." If that is the state of your heart at work, then you are actually enslaving yourself to mammon. Is there another alternative?

Here's a radical idea: Even in the most unpleasant jobs, you have a choice to move psychologically from "making ends meet" to "pursuing higher ends." Even when you are slogging away at a difficult, mundane, or unrewarding job, you can still hone your calling by seeking to develop and use your spiritual gifts. You can view the adversity of undesirable labor as an opportunity to find new gifts, new ways to contribute. You can bring your whole self to work as you try to serve others. It might not make the job fun. But it will make your labor noble, despite how dirty, tired, or ignored you may be. Most importantly, it will make you the master of your work rather than a servant of the demanding idol of mammon.

What If My Calling Doesn't Pay Enough to Live On?

You might feel that your calling draws you to a career that will never pay you enough to make a living. The zookeepers we talked about in Chapter 2, for instance, have mostly accepted that they will never get rich. In fact, most of them hover just above the poverty line.

So, what if you happen to be one of those people whose spiritual gifts don't have a high market value? Is it unwise to persist in doing work that brings financial sacrifice to your family? Is it selfish?

These questions tortured Eli, an extremely bright young man who recently finished his master's degree in management. Eli was a superstar in his program, and then accepted a challenging HR job. After a year, he knew he was in the wrong place. So he left, and made a huge career shift. He became an elementary school teacher for 7- and 8-year olds in a language immersion school.

When Eli talks about his students, his eyes light up. He knows that his teaching really makes a difference. For instance, he worked closely with one particularly belligerent child, and eventually helped him to learn to love school. Clearly, Eli was flourishing in his work. But it wasn't easy. He struggled with unsupportive parents, and the political crosswinds of working with administration. Eli might have been able to manage those challenges, however, if it weren't for the nagging financial strain of raising a family on a teacher's salary.

Eli asked the following burning question: "What if your calling in life won't pay the bills? Is it irresponsible of me to do something I love if I can't comfortably support my family at it?" Eli's question is a very personal one, and it would be presumptuous for us to suggest an easy answer. These types of questions can only be answered by individuals and families as they counsel with each other, and with Heavenly Father through fasting and prayer. So we would like to tread cautiously in our response to Eli and those who share his concerns. But here are some insights we would offer to Eli as he decides what is best for his family.

Response #1

What does it really mean to support a family? If you contrast our luxurious Western lifestyle with that of most people in the world, even our elementary school teachers live in comparative opulence. It could be that our modern perspective on "supporting a family" may be a little warped.

Jeff's father was a high school science teacher. Consequently, Jeff spent his early childhood in a tiny house with very simple means (by US standards). Money was tight, and often a worry. His father took extra jobs to make ends meet. But Jeff did not suffer at all because he didn't have the best toys or the coolest vacations. His childhood felt golden, and he feels he learned perspective, economy, and (hopefully) humility because of his upbringing. In any case, he most certainly benefited from an example of a father who did meaningful work extremely well.

When Stuart was just approaching his teenage years, his father left a comfortable job as a university professor to start a company that was devoted to improving education for children. Although the family supported him, the shift resulted in some very lean years. Food was homegrown, Christmas gifts were hand-made, and vacations were often … well … at home. But there was always food on the table. Christmases and family time together were always magical and memorable. And in the end, the family learned important lessons about economy, simplicity, and sacrificing personal comforts to serve others.

It is tempting to believe that "supporting a family" means providing the luxuries of contemporary life. Parents do have a responsibility to ensure adequate food, shelter, and clothing for their children. But beyond that, the example you set for your children and the spiritual framework you provide is far more important than any exciting vacation, new toy, or luxury. Eli might feel financially limited because of his choice of work, but he probably has adequate means to live modestly and provide for his family's basic material needs.

Response #2

What hidden costs will you incur if you accept lucrative work that you don't love? Eli might be wealthier now if he had stayed on the corporate track. But it probably would have cost him his sense of purpose and some of the energy he could devote to his family. If you are concerned about whether your work gives you enough money to support your kids, give deep consideration to this: how do you weigh the importance of giving your kids money against the importance of giving them your energy, joy, and example?

Response #3

Are you really sure that your calling won't pay off in the long run? You are most likely to excel when your work is a calling. And people who excel usually (though not always) get rewarded in the long term. One of our friends sacrificed tremendously in his early career to pursue nonprofit work that he cared deeply about. There seemed to be few opportunities for upward growth in his small organization. Over time, though, as he poured his heart into his work, he developed a unique set of skills. Larger nonprofits began seeking him out. New job opportunities have come to him, as well as many invitations to work as a guest speaker and educator. Today, he is one of the best-paid nonprofit executives in his region, and makes a very comfortable living.

Of course, not everyone finds ways to become wealthy pursuing their passions. We can't guarantee that your gifts will pay off monetarily. But it is important not to jump to quick conclusions about whether you can "afford" your calling or not.

In conclusion, there are no easy answers to Eli's question. It took much pondering, prayer and counsel for him to decide what he needed to do. (Ultimately, he decided to further his own education so that he could contribute more to the field of education). But our main response to Eli, and to you, is that you shouldn't rush too quickly to abandon your calling because you fear it might not make you rich. When you die, it will be better to have a smile on your lips from the joy of meaningful work than ulcers from toiling unpleasantly to make money. And you will take to your grave exactly the same dollar amount as the wealthiest person in the world.

A Final Note to Brandon

Before we close this chapter, let's return to Brandon, our friend who is unhappy in his foreign ministry consulting job, but who feels trapped because of the financial benefits it provides. It's important to remember that Brandon has consistently made it a matter of prayer when he decides what path to take. So far, the spirit has clearly directed him to stay put. Although Brandon isn't thrilled with that answer, he is willing to obey the promptings.

However, we are very concerned that Brandon might be interpreting the Lord's answer to mean that he should give up on professional happiness altogether. At the risk of being presumptuous, we might suggest to Brandon that perhaps he is not accurately interpreting the Lord's intent.

First off, Brandon is almost certainly taking too short-term a view of the meaning of his work. The Lord can see the full journey whereas we just see down to the curve in the road. In the feature film "The Best Exotic Marigold Hotel," there is a great line delivered by a young hyper-optimistic Indian man. He says, "Here in India we have a saying that everything will be fine in the end. So if everything is not fine, then it is not the end." Humorous as that statement is, there is wisdom in it, especially viewed with eternal eyes. Could it be that Brandon is just paying dues to reach a point where his work does become a true reflection of his spiritual gifts?

We invite Brandon, and you, to exercise faith that the Lord will direct your professional path. Don't become complacent and resigned in your work because you have to make a living. The Lord intends that you use your spiritual gifts to bless His children—whether at work, at church, or at home. There are no areas in your life where He says, "No, I can't really use you there. Just keep your head down and get through that part of your life." In the eternal scheme, we suspect that Brandon isn't in the Middle East to make money, but rather to be honed and shaped for greater service in the Lord's kingdom and to his fellowman. In the eternal perspective, money is just a nice side benefit of work. Using your spiritual gifts to serve is the real reason to work.

What To Do Now

1. Schedule a time to have a conversation with your spouse or someone you respect to discuss your motivations for the work you do (or hope to do). Consider the following questions:

   - What percentage of my chosen career plan is motivated by using my gifts to serve others?
   - What percentage is motivated by financial gain?
   - Have I achieved the right balance between these motives?
   - In what ways am I allowing "mammon" to divert me from the ways I can best serve professionally?
   - What financial sacrifices am I willing to make in order to ensure that I (and my spouse) can render meaningful service at work and at home?

2. Identify a few things about your work that are most meaningful to you. Choose at least one and prepare to talk to your family or friends about it. For example, devote a family home evening to talking about the importance of honest work, and of serving others through your professional career.

Endnotes

1. *The Guardian*, June 17, 2012.

Notes

Notes

Notes

CHAPTER 7

Isn't a Calling Supposed to Be Fun?

CORRECTING HERESY #5:

"WHEN YOU FIND YOUR CALLING, YOUR WORK WILL BE BLISSFUL."

When we first started studying the work life of zookeepers, we thought we had stumbled upon the happiest employees in the world. As we described in Chapter 2, zookeepers have sky-high levels of job satisfaction. They positively ooze enthusiasm when they talk about their animals. So, our first impression of zookeeping was: *This must be a really fun job!*

And we were right.

But we were also very, very wrong.

If you ask zookeepers what is fun about their job, they almost always give the same answers: spending time with the animals, enriching the animals' activities, seeing animals thrive, and participating in animal births (they often get emotional talking about that one). It's impossible not to smile when zookeepers share their infectious love for animals. They are most definitely having fun at work!

But if you ask what *isn't* fun about zookeeping, you also get a lot of immediate and consistent answers. In fact, the list is quite a bit longer: foul smells, unsavory chores, backbreaking labor, working outdoors in bad weather, fighting to get enough resources for your animal, convincing management about what's best for your animals, dealing with disrespect and ignorance from the public, watching animals struggle to survive in captivity, seeing animals get sick, and watching their animals die (they *always* get emotional talking about that one). For zookeepers, there is just as much heartache and heartburn as there are heartwarming experiences. Zookeeping can be brutally difficult.

So, why are zookeepers so consistently happy about their work when they experience so much hardship? Bear in mind that they also receive very small salaries. Why are they so satisfied with their jobs?

The fifth heresy that the world teaches you about meaningful work is that when you find your calling in life, your work will be blissful. The "dream job" phenomenon gives people a sense that somewhere there is an ideal role that will be constantly interesting and exciting. Picture marching off to your job like Snow White's dwarves, whistling a happy tune because you can't wait to work.

Our goal is not to squash that happy dream. Indeed, if you are doing work that allows you to serve others through your spiritual gifts, then you will sometimes have moments of exquisite bliss at work—like the zookeeper we met who witnessed the birth of an extremely endangered breed of rhinoceros. Looking for happiness, fun, and excitement in your work is laudable. Where you get into trouble, though, is when you start to think that if you aren't having a grand old time, you haven't found your calling at all.

Think for a moment about your very favorite pastime. Maybe some recreational activity comes to mind: skiing, hunting, quilting, reading, cooking. You probably get a lot of enjoyment from the activity. But are there parts of it that are toilsome? Skiing is a thrilling pastime. But do you really *enjoy* the experience of lugging your heavy equipment to the resort, or shivering on the chair lift during a blustery day? Reading is a great escape, but you will sometimes run into a tiresome book, or struggle to get through a difficult or mundane passage. No matter what you do for fun, you pay a price for it. In fact, sometimes paying the price makes the activity more fulfilling. For the hunter, the thrill of bagging game is heightened by the intense physical exertion of getting to an animal's remote habitat.

So if the joy of recreation is enhanced by the price you pay for moments of pure fun, why should you think that satisfying work comes with no price? And yet, more and more people seem to be talking about how work should feel like play. This message subtly suggests to the rising generation that their jobs ought to be fun, first and foremost. But that highly simplistic message ignores Lehi's sublime principle that in life, there must be "opposition in all things. If not so... righteousness could not be brought to pass, neither wickedness, neither holiness nor misery, neither good nor bad... [nor] happiness nor misery" (2 Nephi 2:11). It never has been in the Lord's plan for you to get cheap happiness. There is simply no such thing.

So the idea of professional nirvana is actually a hollow dream. The old saying that "if you truly love your job, you will never work a day in your life" is, frankly, baloney. We would love to hear a few more graduation speeches telling the rising generation "It's going to be really tough out there, and you will have to work your tail off, but it will be worth the effort!"

The Price of Meaning

After talking about opposition between good and bad, happiness and misery, Lehi uses an interesting phrase. He teaches that "all things must needs be a compound in one" or they become "as dead" (2 Nephi 2:11). Those are striking words. They suggest, for instance, that your life is only vibrant and animated if it includes a jumbled variety of emotions, pressures, ideas, and experiences. Indeed, if you were happy all the time, you would become "as dead," because you could no longer recognize what happiness is. The blandness of that static condition would eliminate the possibility of joy.

It turns out that the zookeepers in our study understood Lehi's principle well. When we first heard them use the word "calling," we naively assumed they meant that their work was consistently joyful. But as we probed deeper, we realized that they considered their work a calling not *in spite of* hardships, but actually *because of them!* The more they sacrifice, sweat, and suffer to serve their animals, the more meaningful the work becomes, and the more satisfying the successes.

Of course, Lehi is not the only person to have taught the importance of opposition. Joseph Campbell was a professor of literature who studied and taught about hero myths in the 1970s. He found that a pervasive theme, across many cultural hero myths, was that heroes look to their hearts to find their passion and then pursue it. They don't follow money or prestige, but they stay true to an inner compass that compels them to act with integrity, even if they must undertake great suffering and sacrifice for it. Campbell gave a series of widely watched interviews on PBS back in the 1970s, and as part of his message, he coined the phrase "follow your bliss" to describe what motivates heroes.[1] The phrase caught on. It was embraced by young people of the day who were advocating world peace and rejecting many social institutions. It started appearing on bumper stickers, signs, and clothing. Even today, you see the phrase "follow your bliss" everywhere. After some time passed, however, Campbell developed grave misgivings about how people were interpreting the phrase. Heroes, after all, aren't just in it for the pleasure. In some dismay, he quipped, "What I should have said was, 'Follow your blisters!'"

You can't have bliss without blisters. This is true of life in general, and also of your work. You may do the most important, exciting work in the world. But still, some days will be no fun at all. Those days are part of the price you pay to get a sense of meaning at work.

A good example of the price of meaning is Mr. Manning, a junior high music teacher who has been directing his school's choir for seven years. He looks hardly older than some of the kids he conducts. At a recent concert, he led them in a few obligatory pop songs like "Hey There, Delilah" to keep things fresh for the kids. But the bulk of the repertoire leaned more heavily to offerings like "Jesu, Joy of Man's Desiring" and other challenging and beautiful pieces. The musicality may not have been quite ready for Carnegie Hall, but the kids sang with as much heart and conviction as any professional performer.

The reason the students were so committed became obvious near the end of the concert. Mr. Manning took the microphone and spoke about his love for the kids, and his passion for helping them use music to express themselves. Then a flood of alumni came to the stage to join the combined choirs for a final, moving number, followed by a massive group hug with Mr. Manning as nucleus.

Watching people like Mr. Manning excel at their callings in life enriches all of us. Jeff, who was there to watch his daughter perform, reflected, "We who were in the audience left the concert more determined than ever to pour our heart into the things that matter to us. It is impossible to watch Mr. Manning and to not wish to infuse your own work with dedication, love, and service."

But to leave the story there would be a disservice to Mr. Manning. It's very romantic to applaud the maestro at the end of a great performance and think, "Wow, he made that look so easy! He is so gifted!" People don't often pause amidst their applause to weigh the sacrifice, strain, setbacks, frustrations and yes, even moments of despair that usually precede an artistic achievement. You might not give much thought to the financial sacrifices a junior high choir director makes, or to the challenges of working for a lofty cause (like musical education) while having to fight tooth and nail for resources and respect.

Mr. Manning gave some insight into those struggles:

> *"It's been my practice to keep a copy of inspiring feedback such as yours as a supportive reminder in times of trial or difficulty... I have had a number of individuals, some very close to me, who have continually questioned my decision to be a choir teacher. After 7 years of doing it, I have a hard time believing I could be happier elsewhere. Regardless of the great challenges."*

It would be understandable if Mr. Manning became fed up with people questioning his career choice, and left for a job that paid better and provided more recognition. The challenges he faces—both personal and political—are very heavy at times. But even though others may question his career choice, hundreds of students will never doubt that his work matters a great deal—precisely because of what Mr. Manning chooses to put into it, in the face of all the sacrifice and struggle.

Zookeepers—and anyone with a calling—are willing to endure hardship because their work means something. One thing that zookeepers told us really struck this point home. We had a standard interview question: "What would be grounds for divorce from the zoo?" Typically, when researchers ask that question of employees, they will respond with statements like, "Well, if they were mistreating me, I would leave," or "If they weren't paying me what I'm worth, I would look for another job." Most of the zookeepers we talked to, however, answered something like, "There is nothing that would cause me to leave this place." Management neglect? Underpayment? Disrespect? None of that was enough to put zookeepers over the edge and send them packing. One entomologist we asked about "grounds for divorce" responded incredulously, "You mean, other than, like, getting fired?" We knew we were talking to a different breed of employee than the typical office dweller.

So we started following up by asking questions that seemed to cut closer to the heart: "What if the zoo started neglecting or mistreating the animals? Would that be enough to cause you to leave?" The responses to that question were stunning. Here's one typical answer: "If there was any gross misconduct or animal mistreatment or anything like that, I wouldn't... leave the zoo because of that. In fact it would make me try and work harder to solve the problem." It's pretty clear that zookeepers don't consider caring for animals as just a job. Rather, their animals are a stewardship. Even if the zoo was grossly negligent, they would stay in their jobs because it is up to them to protect their animals. You can't really understand what it means to have a calling until you understand what stewardship means.

The Meaning of Stewardship

Let's consider the difference between shepherds and "hirelings," as described in the Bible. Ancient shepherds were devoted to each of their individual sheep, even if there were hundreds in the flock. A good shepherd gave each sheep a name, and cared for it so lovingly that it would come immediately when called. The tenderness of that relationship is one of the reasons that Jesus is called the "Good Shepherd."

But then you have the hireling, which Job describes as a sheepherder that "looketh for the reward of his work" (Job 7:2). In other words, hirelings are in it for the money. They wouldn't bother to form an intimate relationship with the flock, because there is no financial gain in doing so. Instead of beckoning sheep by name, they would rely on their dogs to nip aggressively at the heels of the sheep to keep them moving.

And what does the hireling do when peril arises? Jesus described the hireling's response to a wolf attack: "But he that is an hireling, and not the shepherd, whose own the sheep are not, seeth the wolf coming, and leaveth the sheep, and fleeth: and the wolf catcheth them, and scattereth the sheep. The hireling fleeth, because he is an hireling, and careth not for the sheep" (John 10:12–14).

The zookeepers we studied gave us a better appreciation of the difference between shepherds and hirelings. Zookeepers are modern-day shepherds to their animals. In fact, some zookeepers resent the name "keeper" because it implies that all they do is guard and feed their animals, sort of like a hireling. They prefer the title "animal handler" or "animal caretaker" because it better captures their commitment to the welfare of their animals, a commitment that often leads them to make significant sacrifices. Zookeepers are essentially "on call" at any hour if their animals need assistance, such as when they are ill or birthing. There are not many hirelings who would make that sort of sacrifice, especially for such a low-paying job.

Once you understand stewardship, the "price" of a calling becomes clear. It may be that some people feel stymied in their quest for a personal calling precisely because they aren't prepared for the sort of sacrifice and commitment that only a shepherd understands. Do you see your work as a stewardship—as a "flock" to be lovingly tended? If so, you will be ever ready to put aside your own comfort and convenience to provide the care your flock requires.

Maybe the idea of a "flock" doesn't really ring a bell for you as you think about your work. It might be easy for a doctor to think of her patients as a "flock," or for a teacher to view his students with a "sheep" analogy. But what if you spend your day working with computer screens, tools, diagrams, spreadsheets or raw materials, rather than with people? Can you feel stewardship for inanimate objects?

A lovely poem by W. H. Auden suggests that you can.

> "You need not see what someone is doing
> to know if it is his vocation
>
> you have only to watch his eyes:
> a cook mixing a sauce, a surgeon
>
> making a primary incision,
> a clerk completing a bill of lading,

> wear the same rapt expression, forgetting themselves in a function.
>
> How beautiful it is,
> that eye-on-the-object look."[2]

As Auden artfully illustrates, having a calling (he uses the synonym "vocation") means that you come to care deeply about your craft, your tools, your work products. They are a stewardship to you, just as the master's property was a stewardship in the Savior's parable of the talents. People with a calling pay the price of hardship, sweat, and perseverance in order to fulfill their stewardship to their craft. And, as we learned from Martin Luther, every worthy craft ultimately serves the human family by making the world a better, safer, cleaner, more humane, more educated, or more beautiful place.

Callings don't come cheap! And you don't get to experience the fulfillment of the zookeeper or the shepherd until you are ready to give almost everything for your stewardship. As with everything worthwhile in life, meaningful work comes with a price.

Finding Calling Amidst Drudgery

You may have heard of Mike Rowe, the host of the Discovery Channel's popular series called "Dirty Jobs." In each episode of the show, Rowe works as an apprentice for one day in some job that most people would avoid. During the ten years since the show first aired, Rowe has worked as a sheep castrator, worm dung farmer, sewer inspector, pig farmer, chimney sweeper, avian vomitologist, casino food recycler, and roadkill cleaner, to name just a few of his occupational adventures. As a result of these experiences, Rowe has become a fierce advocate for skilled labor. He has launched a website, has testified before Congress, and has spoken countless times on the dignity and importance of hard, difficult, monotonous labor—labor that has become marginalized and stigmatized in a world that celebrates four-year college degrees and white-collar jobs.

Rowe's core message is that there is nobility and dignity in any honest work, and that hard labor is just as meaningful as the work of the doctor, lawyer, or teacher. Rowe has observed that "People with dirty jobs are happier than you think. As a group, they're the happiest people I know."[3]

It may seem strange that inspecting sewers could be someone's calling. Could anyone really feel passionate about that? In fact, Rowe argues that people who have dirty jobs *didn't* get there by "following their passion." Instead, they saw work that needed to be done and learned how to do so they could make a living. But he also notes that the happiest and most successful of these people never lost sight of their passion or their professional dreams. They simply found different ways of expressing those passions and dreams—perhaps by putting their own creative twist on the work they were doing. As Rowe explains, "one of the things I learned from doing this show was the idea that following your passion is not nearly as important as bringing it along for the ride." What a profound insight! Your inmost passions may not be very evident in the *content* of the work you are doing, but highly evident in *how* you do that work, and for what purpose.

Sometimes, the difference between drudgery and enjoyment at work is a matter of perspective. And sometimes it's a matter of patience. You might expect that your college degree will lead immediately to a great job, or that your talents will quickly open doors for you. With such expectations, you can easily become disappointed when you find yourself doing work that you suspect is beneath you. You might think, "Hey, this work is boring! Something has gone terribly wrong here! I've missed my calling!" And then you go into professional panic mode.

What's ironic about this reaction is that we Latter-day Saints have a pretty strong grasp of the role of adversity in helping our spiritual growth. How often do we share examples about a personal crisis or family trial turning us to our Heavenly Father and deepening our reliance upon Him? And yet—perhaps because our jobs are a matter of financial necessity—we rarely think about a trying job being *good* for our long-term career development. The fact is that you can learn wonderful lessons from jobs that are hard, frustrating, boring, or even painful. As we mentioned earlier, miserable jobs teach you a lot about who you *aren't*, so that you are better equipped to make future choices that align your work with your gifts. But more than that, difficult jobs sometimes become a crucible of refinement that allow you to develop resilience and strength. The fact that difficult jobs humble you is a reason to be thankful for them.

In the spirit of "opposition in all things," can you really come to appreciate a calling in life if you haven't experienced the *lack* of calling? Could it be that your painful work experiences are merciful gifts from your Heavenly Father that will increase your capacity for fulfillment in later chapters of your life?

The scriptures actually instruct us about how to handle grueling, unsatisfying work. Consider the people of Alma, who were virtually enslaved by Amulon, the former priest whom the Lamanites had made a ruler over them. He heaped heavy burdens upon them and persecuted them with oppressive labor. Alma's people were not even allowed to pray vocally, but they poured out their hearts secretly to Heavenly Father to ask for His help. Their prayers were answered, but not with an immediate release from their labors. Rather, the Lord promised to "ease the burdens which are put on your shoulders, that even you cannot feel them upon your backs" (Mosiah 24:14). This promise was fulfilled, and Alma's people found themselves easily capable to meet the physical demands of their work. No doubt they still didn't find it enjoyable, but they "submitted cheerfully and with patience" to the Lord's will and to the labor they were required to do (Mosiah 24:15).

CALLING

You are probably unlikely to experience actual enslavement as part of your career. So no matter how lousy your work seems, you can always look to Alma's people as an example of faith and perseverance in an even worse professional position than you will ever occupy. Like Alma's people, you may sometimes feel a bit trapped in a role. You might feel that you have too little discretion or autonomy at work. Like them, you might hope for a future "deliverance" from your job. Like them, you might find your work terribly taxing—perhaps even unfair.

But, also like Alma's people, you can respond to feelings of entrapment with faith and diligence. Even if you can't perceive how your professional lot in life could ever improve, you can "submit cheerfully and with patience" to your occupational demands, and put your faith in the Lord's purposes for your life. When you exercise that sort of faith in the Lord, you will see that He also "eases the burdens" on your back.

The Savior taught us that "my yoke is easy, and my burden is light" (Matthew 11:30). But an easy yoke is still a yoke, and a light burden is still a burden. As with the people of Alma, waiting patiently on the Lord, and "submitting cheerfully" is precisely what He expects of us before He opens new and glorious opportunities.

Submitting cheerfully *doesn't* mean becoming passive and defeatist. The people of Alma didn't give up on the Lord, or resign themselves to perpetual enslavement. Rather, they exercised patience, which implies not resignation, but hope. Consequently, if you feel unhappily stuck in a position or a career, resigning yourself to years of bitterness while you wait for retirement is probably not the Lord's will for you. Instead, these scriptures suggest that you patiently—and hopefully—do the best you can, cheerfully serving and vigilantly seeking for the hand of the Lord to reveal the next opportunity He has in store for you.

An Example of Submitting Cheerfully

Our friend Sam is a great example of how patiently doing all you can in the midst of a less-than-exciting career can open doors to something more fulfilling. After his family sold the business that he had co-owned throughout his early adulthood, Sam struggled to find work that would both provide for his family and give him a sense of professional achievement. Eventually, Sam found some success by building a small business. He finished concrete floors—usually in residential garages. Although there was adequate demand for his skills, the work was repetitive and didn't provide Sam the sense of challenge he longed for. The job also required Sam to continually "pound the pavement" for new customers. Going door to door was the only way he could maintain his livelihood since his job provided no opportunity for repeat customers. As Sam put it, "I was firing myself after each job I finished."

Sam kept at his business for six years, getting by—sometimes just barely—but never feeling like he was doing what he loved, or providing for his family in the way that he wanted to. How would Sam ever find his calling while he was stuck finishing floors? At one particularly low point, Sam asked his stake president for a blessing to help him know how to provide better for his family. The blessing gave him some very pointed assurances—including that he need not worry, and that the Lord would soon provide Sam a way not only to make a comfortable living, but also to help others in the process.

One day soon after the blessing, Sam was hired to finish the floors of a cabin belonging to a man named Rob, who is a successful entrepreneur. As they drove up the canyon together, Sam inquired what business Rob was currently working on. Rob described a new venture that involved providing social media services to companies through Facebook and other internet-based platforms. Sam was intrigued by the company's product, and immediately started thinking about business owners he knew who might be interested. Sam told Rob, "I think

I can sell that!" Rob appreciated Sam's enthusiasm but explained that he already had a sales team in place and didn't have a spot for a new person.

Undeterred, Sam started talking to his various contacts about the new business anyway. And here is where Sam's spiritual gifts started to surface in a significant way. You need to know that Sam is extremely gifted at connecting with people and forming relationships. He describes himself as the type of person who can't stand by in an elevator without striking up a conversation with a fellow rider. Sam's friends affectionately refer to him as "The Mayor," because wherever he goes, he seems to run into someone in the community that he knows. So it wasn't much of a stretch for Sam to believe that he could find people who would share his enthusiasm for the new business idea.

Within a few months, Sam had brought so many new clients—including some very large ones—into Rob's business that Rob really had no choice but to hire him. By his second month of employment, Sam was the most successful salesman in the company. The job gave Sam a sparkle in his eye. He has taken a huge step toward his calling in life.

But when Sam looks back on his years as a floor finisher, he feels it was a necessary preparation for him. Finishing floors gave him a commitment to meticulousness that has enhanced his professionalism. Selling his services door-to-door built his confidence in approaching potential clients. And, of course, Sam never would have found his current job if he hadn't finished the floor of his boss' cabin.

As he reflects back on the years of struggling as he searched for his calling, Sam said,

> *"The Lord is involved in our lives in the smallest, simplest ways, and we don't even realize it. The question is whether we have that childlike faith to see it. Instead of questioning whether it's the hand of the Lord or not, we just need to say, 'yeah, that was the Lord.'"*

It would have been easy for Sam to think that God had forgotten him when he was struggling for years with his floor-finishing business. And there were probably times when Sam's faith wavered. But in retrospect, Sam can now see how his Heavenly Father was refining him through those challenging times to prepare him to do work that allows him to use his best gifts.

Bliss and Blisters

When you look at people who do meaningful work, you tend to focus on the fun stuff. It's easy to develop a romantic notion of zookeepers cuddling up with exotic species, but most of us don't appreciate the backbreaking, sometimes smelly, and occasionally heartbreaking aspects of their work. Despite blisters, however, many people remain aglow about their work. Bliss and blisters, it turns out, aren't opposites. In fact, they are two sides of the same coin.

In all of this, however, you must remember that happiness is not just about your occupational circumstances. When you live righteously, you can experience true happiness even if your job isn't thrilling. On the other hand, if you stray from the commandments, even the most fascinating career won't prevent you from feeling misery. Happiness is far more about *how* you live (and work) than about what happens to you along the way. And honest, diligent labor—even if it's menial—is part of the Lord's recipe for happiness. Nephi's people, for instance, "did sow seed, and… raise flocks… build buildings, and… work in all manner of wood, and of iron, and of copper, and of brass, and of steel, and of gold, and of silver…" (2 Nephi 5:11, 15). All of that labor was part of living "after the manner of happiness." (2 Nephi 5:27).

Going back to Adam and Eve's dismissal from the Garden of Eden, it's obvious that our mortal work was not meant to be easy. In fact, we humans don't deeply appreciate things when they come easy for us. That's why the bike your grandmother gave you as a child might have sat neglected and rusty in your shed, but the one you bought with your own hard-earned money stayed shiny for years. So those hard knocks, unpleasant jobs, and false starts on your career path may just be necessary ingredients to your future joy. We invite you to banish the heretical idea that dream jobs are fun every day, and that bliss comes from a lack of blisters. That worldly doctrine is a page out of the adversary's blueprint: pleasure without price. Followers of the Savior know that only sacrifice "brings forth the blessings of heaven" (Praise to the Man, Hymn #27).

What To Do Now

1. Reflect on the ways in which you have "paid your dues" in life. List sacrifices you have made (and continue to make) on behalf of your professional career. Then enumerate blessings and benefits that have come from each of these sacrifices. Record in your journal your reflections on how the hardships you have faced have influenced your professional life. Evaluate whether these sacrifices have been worth the benefits that you received.

2. Talk to someone who is working in a position or profession that you might be interested in pursuing in the future. Ask the following types of questions:

    a. What is the hardest thing about your work?

    b. What do you enjoy least about the work you do?

    c. What sacrifices did you/do you make in order to pursue your profession?

    d. How have hardships and sacrifices influenced the way you feel about your job? Has it been worth it?

3. Have a conversation with your spouse or a trusted friend or relative about the price you are willing to pay in order to pursue work that

you love to do. Evaluate how the hardships associated with your desired profession will impact your family, your church service, and your spirituality. Consider ways in which those hardships might strengthen you, and increase your capacity as a spouse, parent, and servant to others. Discuss whether these prices are ones your family is willing and able to pay.

Endnotes

1. See Joseph Campbell with Bill Moyers. 1988. *The Power of Myth*, edited by Betty Sue Flowers. New York: Doubleday
2. Auden, W. H. 2007. *Selected Poems* (expanded Second Edition). Vintage.
3. Mike Rowe TED Talk: "Learning from dirty jobs." Posted online March 2009.

Notes

CHAPTER 8

Callings and Fame

**CORRECTING HERESY #6:
"WHEN YOU FIND YOUR CALLING, THE WORLD WILL TAKE NOTICE."**

Barb was a custodian at the first university where Jeff taught. She was a tiny dynamo of a woman, probably in her mid-50s. Despite her less-than-glamorous position, she had a huge impact on Jeff. He recalls:

> *Every afternoon Barb came into my office, a smiling flurry of activity, to take out my trash. She often asked if there was some special task she might do to make my office cleaner. I couldn't bring myself to ask her to do more menial labor than she already had to do. So I never took her up on her offer. But in time, I came to realize that she really did want to do more for me. Her offer was sincere.*
>
> *I became fascinated about why Barb tackled her work with such gusto, and with such a big smile on her face. One day I asked her, "Barb, how do you feel about your job?" I guess I shouldn't have been surprised at her response.*
>
> *She beamed. "I love it," she said. "I'm happy to be part of this school and I really love trying to make it a better place. Plus," she added proudly, "I'm really good at what I do."*
>
> *And she was right. Barb did make the university a better place. As I thought about her answer, I realized that her work*

had a more important impact on me than just keeping my trash emptied. Her enthusiasm made me want to be a better professor. I wanted to bring Barb's brand of devoted excellence to my own work. And I felt like I somehow owed it to Barb—and to the many hardworking people like her—to do my part to make the university a better place too.

I never expressed any of that to Barb. I regret that now, because she deserved to hear how much her example impacted me.

The Fame Heresy

It is tempting to equate fame with greatness. Even in the Church, people sometimes talk of General Authorities and General Officers as if they were celebrities, or possessed superhuman qualities. We once spoke to a seasoned stake presidency member who had rubbed shoulders with many great Church leaders, all of whom seemed to shine in the spotlight of public admiration. When we asked what it was like to interact with such amazing people, he responded, "The greatest people I have ever met in the Church are the clerks and secretaries." He explained that these quiet servants consecrate countless hours of labor to maintain the organization of wards and stakes. They do so faithfully, without complaint, and generally without fanfare from the people whose lives they most bless.

Those words were humbling. We realized that, in asking our question, we had unwittingly equated greatness with fame. We had fallen for the twisted logic of the sixth heresy of work: that when you find your calling in life, you will know it by the way the world celebrates it.

The Savior teaches us: "But when thou doest alms, let not thy left hand know what thy right hand doeth: That thine alms may be in secret: and thy Father which seeth in secret himself shall reward thee openly" (Matthew 6:3–4). The service you render in your working life probably goes unnoticed and unappreciated by the media, the public, or even close associates. But your service always catches the notice of Heavenly Father. According to these verses, His eternal rewards are *more* liberal when you receive no public recognition. When you serve with a self-congratulatory flourish, on the other hand, you cash in the rewards of service immediately; you receive those rewards in the currency of public heroism. But if you forget yourself in serving others in quiet and steady ways, you are treasuring up heavenly rewards. As tennis legend (and quiet mentor) Arthur Ashe put it, "True heroism is remarkably sober, very undramatic. It is not the urge to surpass all others at whatever cost, but the urge to serve others at whatever cost."[1]

Prestige is a telestial concept. The Savior's life provides many examples of His rejection of worldly hierarchies. Although he recognized political authority ("Render to Caesar the things that are Caesar's"; Mark 12:17), he spent much of his time with people who lived in obscurity. His teachings were replete with references to shepherds, fishermen, farmers, homemakers, and other laborers. He celebrated the widow's mite more than the sizeable donations of the wealthy (Mark 12:41–44). He taught that one designated as the master ought to be the servant of others (John 13:13–15). When his disciples quibbled over seating arrangements at the Last Supper, he adjured them not to be like those who "exercise authority," but rather taught that "he that is the greatest among you, let him be as the younger; and he that is chief, as he that doth serve" (Luke 22:26). Throughout His ministry, Jesus chastised the hypocrisy of those who loved "the uppermost rooms at feasts, and the chief seats in the synagogues, and greetings in the markets, and to be called of men, Rabbi, Rabbi" (Matthew 23:6–7). It's a bit puzzling, then, that we who seek to follow the Savior sometimes convince ourselves to choose a profession because it will bring us the honors of men.

Of course, if you excel at your calling in life, you may indeed end up becoming famous. That could prove to be more of a challenge than a blessing. As Orson Scott Card—a person whose work has brought great fame—once observed, "There are some careers in which fame and success cannot be separated." In such careers, striking the right balance becomes especially important, and particularly challenging. He continues:

> "It is very easy in such careers, to start measuring your success by the amount of fame or honors you receive. Fame is like nicotine: Even a single dose can set up a dependency. Many begin to shape their lives in order to get more and bigger hits of fame. Speaking as one who has had a little bit of splash in a very small pond, I have seen how the hunger for awards and recognition and fame—'the honors of men'—sours the lives of those who can never get enough of it. And you can never get enough of it. Why? Because the thrill of fame lasts about 15 seconds, and then it's gone. Or else you start to believe the praise and think you deserve it—not your work, you—which leads to a sense of entitlement that makes you miserable to live with. Our job—whether we're in a fame-inducing career or not—is to do the best work we can, in both senses of 'best': best in quality of workmanship, and best in moral value to those who receive it. Those who do good work will usually have the respect of those who know what good work is. If you aspire to do good things and do them well, then respect will come from those whose respect is worth having."[2]

Pres. Dieter F. Uchtdorf taught this same principle in General Conference in October 2010 when he shared an experience he had with Pres. James E. Faust. He said,

> "President Faust took the time to teach me some important principles about my assignment. He explained also how gracious the members of the Church are, especially to General Authorities. He

said, 'They will treat you very kindly. They will say nice things about you.' He laughed a little and then said, 'Dieter, be thankful for this. But don't you ever inhale it.'

In the very moment you "inhale" the glory of the world, you begin to lose your life's calling. That's because a calling is about what you are equipped to give, not what you feel entitled to receive. As educators, we confess that we have occasionally succumbed to those moments of inhaling. It's tempting to strive for popularity in the classroom by being as likeable as possible and going easy on students. Inevitably, that strategy fails. You end up being less effective as a teacher when you are simply trying to get people to like you, and you start to lose the joy in it. We have learned that when we prioritize loving our students—even when love requires sternness—we are much better teachers, and much happier ones as well.

Finding Nobility in Any Kind of Work

One way to inoculate yourself against the lure of fame is by paying attention to the greatness that surrounds you in your working world. Celebrating others' excellence is one of the surest ways to combat self-absorption.

As the Lord instructs, "let every man stand in his own office, and labor in his own calling; and let not the head say unto the feet it hath no need of the feet; for without the feet how shall the body be able to stand? Also the body hath need of every member, that all may be edified together, that the system may be kept perfect" (D&C 84:109–110). We learn from this doctrine that there is no preeminence to any calling (ecclesiastical or professional). In fact, no system (whether it be a company, a ward, or a family) can achieve its potential without the contributions of *all* of its members, no matter how lowly their position might seem. Think about the implications of that principle! It means that if you feel self-important about what you do, you are *undermining* your organization, rather than contributing to it. There is perhaps no better way to shed your starry-eyed infatuation with prestige than to develop a keen eye for the greatness that others exhibit.

Let's consider, for instance, what we can learn about professional callings from people who are doing work that the world looks down upon. Our colleagues Blake Ashforth and Glen Kreiner published a classic article while they were both at Arizona State University in which they described how people deal with "dirty work." Drawing upon dozens of studies of marginalized occupations, they concluded that people in under-appreciated professions often develop a deep sense of purpose in their work. They do this by emphasizing the positive value they provide and focusing on things they enjoy about their tasks. For instance, they cite research showing that many meat-cutters take pleasure in their specialized skills, many prison guards take pride in their service to society, many dogcatchers view their work as protecting citizen safety, and many gravediggers relish physical activity in the outdoors while they are helping the bereaved.[3]

You may have seen the blockbuster film "The Help," or read Kathryn Stockett's wonderful book that inspired it. It is a compelling account of the battle for dignity in the midst of "dirty work." If you aren't familiar with the story, it's a 1950s tale of black women in the Deep South who are domestic workers ("the help") for white middle-class women who treat them as if they were mindless or invisible. When a white journalist invites these domestic servants to tell about their experiences for a book she is writing, the women decide to divulge their stories to a national audience, despite risks to their safety. Those stories are unforgettable.

Take Aibileen, an aging domestic worker who has lovingly raised many white children, only to see them grow up to be as condescending to her as their parents are. In the story, Aibileen is a far better mother to the toddler she tends than the girl's real mother will ever be. And Aibileen's knowledge of cleaning and housekeeping is so extensive that she becomes the anonymous source for a local newspaper column.

Even though others degrade her, Aibileen is actually fulfilling her calling in life—doing her work with such mastery and originality that the world *ought* to take notice. But instead, she is dismissed, derided, and humiliated. Maybe that's why Aibileen was willing to tell her story. She just wanted to be heard.

Aibileen reminds us of the unprecedented response we received when we started surveying zookeepers, another under-appreciated group. Usually, it's like pulling teeth to get people to fill out surveys about their work. But the zookeepers practically fell over themselves to tell us about what they do. We had never seen such a strong response to a survey. It made us realize that all people, even the ones who do menial labor, tend to view their work as a compelling personal drama—a story that needs to be told. Whether they love their jobs, hate their jobs, or feel something in between, they almost always express strong emotion when you talk to them about what their work *means* to them.

So, one of the ways you can honor the work that people do is to ask them about it. When was the last time you asked a hotel maid about what she does? Or a street sweeper? A temp? You might shy away from talking to people about work when their jobs seem mundane. However, showing genuine interest in someone else's work is one of the best ways to honor it. Your interest may ignite a spark. It might help others recognize their own contributions, and return to their work with increased dedication and focus.

Stuart learned an important lesson about the power of unnoticed work at his university. As he recalls:

In the Executive Education Center where I often teach, there are a lot of good people who work hard doing things that others usually take for granted: sweeping the floors, serving the food, cleaning the classrooms, etc. It occurred to me a few years ago that I had been going about my own business without really noticing these people. It was a painful realization, especially since I believe so strongly in the nobility of all work, so I set a goal to get to know these employees better, to learn their names, to find out a little bit about each one, and to visit with them before class or during breaks.

My goal proved to be an extremely rewarding investment—for me more than for anyone else. One of the employees I befriended was a man named Leonard who works for the custodial staff. Leonard would come in during breaks between classes to clean up around each student's seat. He did an excellent job. I began to notice that Leonard always had a smile and a good word to share: "Hey, my man! How you doin'?" I also noticed that Leonard didn't reserve this treatment for faculty; he greeted everyone the same way, even when they seemed too busy to acknowledge him or engage in conversation with him.

I ran into Leonard one day when I was preparing to teach my class, and we struck up a conversation. Leonard told me, with some pride, that he was celebrating his 10th anniversary in his position that very day—a decade of faithful service, a decade of behind-the-scenes efforts to make the university more livable. Of course, when a faculty member reaches some important milestone (like receiving tenure, getting promoted, or receiving an endowed chair), universities tend to make a big deal of it. But I suspected that Leonard's milestone would come and go with perhaps a pat on the back and a "keep up the good work" from his supervisor, and not much more. And yet he didn't seem to mind—he seemed to genuinely enjoy serving others through his work.

I asked Leonard to come in at the beginning of my class so that the students could recognize him. Leonard hemmed and hawed and said he would try, but he didn't come. For someone *who is accustomed to working behind the scenes, perhaps the idea of that sort of recognition was uncomfortable. So, during a break, I tracked down Leonard's supervisor and asked him to persuade Leonard to come into class after the break.*

Leonard finally did show up as the class was set to resume after the break. He seemed a bit shy and very self-conscious. I had Leonard stand at the front of this class of high-powered Executive MBA students. I reminded the class that Leonard was the one who made sure the classroom looked nice. Across the classroom, there was a sea of nodding heads and smiles of recognition and appreciation. I told the class that today was Leonard's 10-year anniversary as an employee of the university. The students burst into cheers and applause, standing to recognize his dedicated service. Grinning shyly, Leonard mumbled a few words of thank you. It had been his pleasure to serve, he assured the class. He then quickly excused himself and left the room.

Clearly, Leonard wasn't counting on a standing ovation, nor was it the reason that he did his work so cheerfully and conscientiously. But I hope that it meant something to him and wasn't just embarrassing. It certainly reminded the students and me how much we gain from dedicated people who do their work behind the scenes and do it with a smile and a sense of pride.

But other than the simple decency of recognizing other people, there is another reason to stop and celebrate the Leonards of the world. Drawing attention to excellence doesn't simply reward the person who offered their best. It elevates those who give the recognition, and those who hear it. The philosopher David Norton referred to this principle as the "complementarity of excellences." He argued that this principle "affirms that every genuine excellence benefits by every other genuine excellence. It means that the best within every person calls upon and requires the best within every other person."[4] In other words, excellence breeds excellence, so you should look for it everywhere you can.

Taking it a step further, perhaps it's not even *possible* to achieve excellence without inspiration from others. When you neglect to notice the outstanding work of a custodian, you are denying yourself the opportunity learn from him or her. Whenever you see *anyone* performing their calling with devotion, artistry, panache, or brilliance, you will naturally feel an urge to elevate your own contributions through your calling.

Jeff recently encountered a surprising example of excellence breeding excellence in an unlikely place: the clothing issue desk in the men's locker room at BYU. Although customer service on the BYU campus is generally outstanding, he had noticed that the staff at the men's locker room equipment issue desk sometimes seemed like moody adolescents rather than customer service personnel. They tended to sit hunched over their laptops playing games, and seemed mildly annoyed if you interrupted them. They generally didn't make eye contact with the public. In fact, they sometimes offered no more than a grunt when they handed you a clean towel after a workout.

Of course, it's tough to blame them for being less than enthusiastic about their work. A men's locker room isn't exactly a glamorous place. But that's what makes Noah so remarkable. Jeff recalls:

> *I met Noah, one of the locker room staff, a few years ago when I first rented a locker. Noah was a tall, affable student with a big smile and a very respectful manner. I mentioned to him that I was disappointed that the lockers were too small for my racquetball racquet to fit in them. Noah said, "Here, I've got just the ticket." Then he showed me to the back of the room where a top-tier locker happened to be missing a ceiling panel, allowing a racquet to fit snugly inside. I thought, "Wow, this guy is different than the others."*

The next time I came to the locker room, Noah greeted me by my first name. I was really surprised because I hadn't ever introduced myself; Noah had just remembered my name from the locker rental contract. In fact, every time I came in, Noah greeted me personally. He asked me questions about my work and family. Eventually, I began to ask Noah questions about himself too. We became friends, and I was genuinely sad when Noah disappeared one spring after graduating.

Noah, and people like him, are inspiration-givers. Working in one of the least appealing jobs on campus, he brought dignity, professionalism, and genuine service to his work. Jeff was just one of many of his "customers" that he treated as friends. The contrast between him and his aloof colleagues was striking.

It seems unlikely that working in a locker room represents Noah's calling in life. Even so, Noah was using this job to hone his talents and to serve others. He was making the most of a pretty crummy job. In fact, Jeff recently caught up with Noah again, and he assured Jeff that he actually really enjoyed that job. Noah's satisfaction had more to do with what he brought to his work than with the circumstances that surrounded him. Noah is a great example of nobility at work where you might least expect it.

Noah's outgoing nature made it easy to notice his devotion to his work. What would happen, though, if you were always *looking* for ways to celebrate other people's excellences? Noticing other people's spiritual gifts at work emboldens them to use those gifts even more. When you look for nobility in other people's work, you actually help them find and express their calling in life.

As Christians, what is our responsibility toward the Aibileens, Leonards, and Noahs of the world? The Savior saw divine potential and eternal worth in "the least of these" as he ministered to the ignored and invisible. Do you sometimes look right through the clerk, the custodian or the food service worker? Are you missing opportunities to be inspired by their excellence because you are caught up in your own professional importance? Are you missing opportunities to bring out the best in them—to help them recognize their own spiritual gifts—because you see their work as menial or unskilled? As followers of the Savior, we should consider these questions carefully. If not, we run the risk of demeaning our brothers and sisters who offer their callings in less-glamorous ways by treating them as minor cast members in the great drama of our own professional lives. Doing so might just make us modern-day Pharisees.

The Peril of Worldly Labels

When you meet someone new, what questions do you ask? You probably don't get too far into the conversation before asking something like, "What do you do for a living?"

There's nothing unreasonable about that question. After all, people spend a huge percentage of their time working, so defining yourself by your position makes some sense. But when you ask someone about her job title, you also tend to make some quick and convenient judgments about status. In Japan, for instance, this process is highly ritualized. When the Japanese exchange business cards, they know how deeply to bow based on their counterpart's seniority in their organization. In Western culture, we don't stand quite as much on ceremony, but we still tend to assign importance based on people's answer to the "what work do you do?" question. Your demeanor might change suddenly, for instance, if someone you thought was an executive tells you that he is an administrative assistant.

Because we live in such a complex world, using labels to simplify things is absolutely necessary. If you couldn't categorize things around you, your brain might explode from overloading. So, although it may not be fair to pigeonhole someone based on a simple job title, it appears to be an unavoidable reality of human nature that we assign status at the drop of a hat.

Our cognitive hardwiring doesn't excuse us, however, from the Savior's commandment to love all of His children. As we have already mentioned, prestige is a telestial phenomenon. The Savior paid no heed at all to status distinctions in his personal relationship. So why should you permit professional labels to determine how much attention and respect you pay to someone? Alma 1:26 describes how the priests (clearly the most prestigious people in that society) worked shoulder-to-shoulder with laborers who were earning their keep, "and thus they were all equal, and they did all labor, every man according to his strength." For righteous societies, there is no shame or lowliness in getting your hands dirty in honest labor.

John Calvin echoed this principle when he taught, "No task will be so sordid and base . . . that it will not shine and be reckoned very precious in God's sight."[5] Another influential religious figure, Cotton Mather said this:

"Let not a proud heart make you ashamed of that business wherein you may be a blessing. For my part, I can't see an honest man hard at work in the way of his occupation, be it never so mean (and though, perhaps, driving of a wheel barrow) but I find my heart sensibly touched with respect for such a man."[6]

Think how many labor disputes and how much social upheaval would be avoided if everyone treated all work with the respect Calvin and Mather prescribe.

And yet in society, titles and labels become proof of success. People spend arduous years working for a promotion that gives them a prestigious title. They covet the executive parking spot, the corner office, or a salary that allows them to drive a jealousy-inducing sports car. But when people pursue notoriety for its own sake, they don't have much time left over for real service.

In fact, striving for worldly acclaim might be the biggest deterrent there is to finding your calling in life. When you target notoriety and prestige as your primary goal, it is almost impossible to discover your spiritual gifts. Here's why:

The pursuit of prestige actually *contradicts* your inner divinity. The Savior expressed this contradiction in his teaching about treasures. In Matthew, chapter 6, he describes the way some hypocrites would fast—by showing just how miserable they felt so that other men would honor their sacrifice. Of these self-absorbed pretenders, he said, "They have their reward." Then, in a similar vein, he goes on to teach, "Lay not up for yourselves treasures upon earth, where moth and rust doth corrupt, and where thieves break through and steal: But lay up for yourselves treasures in heaven, where neither moth nor rust doth corrupt, and where thieves do not break through or steal" (Matthew 6:19–20). Here, the Savior presents you with a choice about when you get your rewards—now, in the telestial present, or in a celestial eternity.

Consequently, the alluring prestige of the world is actually a cheap (and temporary) substitute for the glory that Heavenly Father has in store for you. If you bask in mortal glory for its own sake—by coveting fame, applause, and approval—you become like the prodigal son who wishes for your inheritance now. Like him, you will ultimately discover that immediate gratification brings long-lasting regret. When you seek to bring glory to yourself now, you are borrowing against a future reward that will leave you nothing but a worthless substitute.

But there is another reason that worldly prestige is contrary to your divine nature. And that reason has to do with one of the most common tools of the adversary: the application of labels. In fact, he is the ultimate master of applying labels to deceive us. Satan attempted to use his labeling trick to distract Moses from his divine destiny. After

Moses had received a grand vision of the Father, and an assurance of his divine sonhood, the adversary immediately arrived to tempt him. Satan's invitation was, "Moses, *son of man*, worship me" (Moses 1:12). By using a subtle label to categorize Moses as a mere mortal, Satan tried to call into question Moses' potential, and to focus his mind on worldly rewards rather than eternal promises. Satan's pattern hasn't changed much since then. He uses worldly labels, and your own insecurities, to lure you into relying upon worldly affirmations of your worth.

Notice how labels come to define people in ways that limit them. Educators formally label some children as "gifted," which imposes expectations of consistent brilliance on some, and suggestions of inferiority on children who aren't thus labeled. Psychologists might label you an "introverts," which could convince you that, try as you might, you don't have the potential to become socially graceful. And society has staunchly insisted on labeling those who experience same-sex attraction simply as "gay," which imposes an artificially black-and-white distinction about how human beings experience sexuality. That label, in particular, places a large percentage of Heavenly Father's children into a category that gives them a fatalistic sense that they don't have much choice about whether they can follow God's laws of chastity.

Of course, most of these labels were not developed with the intent to diminish or limit people. And (as we have suggested) categorization and labeling is essential to surviving in a complex world. However, there is really only one label in the universe that accurately captures your destiny, and that is "child of God." When you fully embrace that one true identity, you liberate yourself from the tyranny of worldly labels. This is a bold claim for a book about finding your calling in life, but we believe that you *can't experience your calling in life until you reject worldly prestige and root your identity in your eternal worth.* Otherwise, you will spend your career chasing the elusive and fleeting praise of man rather than using your unique spiritual gifts to serve.

Losing Your Title to Find Your Calling

Michael Gates Gill is a great example of learning about the hollowness of prestige. He is the author of the bestseller "How Starbucks Saved My Life." Jeff recently spent an afternoon with Michael at the Manhattan Starbucks where his remarkable story unfolded. At 72, Michael has a youthful enthusiasm for the work he does—which might surprise you, since he left the lofty heights of corporate America to work as a barista at Starbucks.

When he was in his 50s, Michael was a well-paid advertising executive, living the high life in Manhattan, and raising a beautiful family. But that life was shattered when Michael got a pink slip from his agency. He was suddenly unemployed. Shortly thereafter, his marriage fell apart and he was diagnosed with a brain tumor. He spent a decade trying to regain his professional footing, but discovered that he couldn't compete with the newly minted MBAs flooding the job market. Ad agencies wanted young faces and fresh ideas. Michael couldn't get back into the game. Eventually, he fell into despair and desperation. How would he support himself? How would he get health insurance to cover his medical needs?

Sitting despondently in a Starbucks in upper Manhattan one day, Michael was mistaken for a job applicant. He thought to himself, "Why not? At least I would have health benefits." He applied and was hired as a barista. Thus began an astonishing journey of professional awakening.

Truly humbled by his circumstances, Michael decided to throw himself into his Starbucks job, even though it seemed somehow "beneath him." He soon found that he took pride in keeping the restroom immaculately clean. He got to know the customers personally and befriended them. He swallowed his fear of the cash register and learned the skill of cashiering. He discovered, to his surprise, that he was happier serving coffee than he had ever been in his corporate career.

Michael was also awestruck by the qualities and the dedication of

Callings and Fame

his coworkers—people he previously would have ignored if he passed them on the street. And he discovered that the business of serving coffee was a business of love—providing something that warms and nurtures people. He found a dimension of meaning and importance in his work at Starbucks that he had never experienced on the fast-track of corporate self-absorption.

When Jeff met with him, Michael shared some powerful reflections that don't appear in his book. In recent years, Michael has developed a deepened sense of spirituality about his professional journey. During the time of his career crisis, he didn't think much about God. But now he attributes the twists and turns of his journey to the hand of God. Even though he weathered devastating professional, family, and health crises, he is now full of gratitude, because those setbacks taught him how to relish life and find lasting satisfaction. For Michael, getting laid off was a blessing—a merciful re-tracking of his life that revealed to him the superficiality of his prestigious career. When he awakened to the nobility of his coworkers, he gained a stronger sense of what he had to offer the world. Ironically, he had to lose prestige to find meaning.

Michael doesn't think that serving coffee is what defines his calling in life. As of this writing, he still works at Starbuck and loves his job. But what gives him the deepest sense of purpose is telling his story through writing and public speaking. *That* is Michael's calling. And he never would have arrived here without that pink slip that knocked him off his glamorous perch.

Is there a way that you can learn to reject the sixth heresy without paying the sort of price Michael had to pay? Equating your calling with prestige is precisely the recipe for *not* discovering your calling in life. If you put service first, however, and recognize the nobility of all work, you are much more likely to discover the work you were meant to do, and to avoid the deceptive, hollow temptations of the "great and spacious building" that is the prestige of the world.

What to Do Now

1. Think of at least a couple of people near where you work or live who do menial or underappreciated work. Try to think of people you have never spoken with before. Find an opportunity to strike up a conversation with one or two of these individuals. Express interest in their work and appreciation for what they contribute. Record in your learning journal the insights you gained from these conversations.

2. Think of a few colleagues you work closely with, or have worked closely with in the past. Carefully consider what unique qualities they brought to their work. What evidence of spiritual gifts did you observe in them? Write a note to one of these people describing the particular strength you have observed and thanking him or her for the example and inspiration.

3. Engage in deep reflection about how much the praise of the world matters to you in your professional life. Ask yourself the following questions: Would I still want to do the work that I do if I didn't receive praise and recognition? If I knew that my current (or desired) line of work would never bring me fame and prestige, would it change my desire to do it? What parts of my work do I do only because of the worldly attention they bring to me? Record the insights you gained as you honestly asked yourself these questions.

4. Identify someone who you deeply respect for his or her professional service. Ask to have a conversation with this individual about his or her motivations at work. Ask this person to share with you feelings about how (or whether) the approval of the world shaped his or her career decisions. Listen carefully and record what you learn in your journal.

Endnotes

1. Quoted in Kelly, B. 2003. *Worth Repeating: More Than 5,000 Classic and Contemporary Quotes.* Kregel.
2. Card, O. S. 2009. Seek to be worthy of praise. *Deseret News.* August 20.
3. Ashforth, B. E. & Kreiner, G. E. 1999. "How Can You Do It?": Dirty Work and the Challenge of Constructing a Positive Identity. *Academy of Management Review,* 24(3): 413–434.
4. Norton, D. L. 1976. *Personal Destinies: A Philosophy of Ethical Individualism.* Princeton University Press. Page 10.
5. John Calvin, The Institutes of the Christian Religion, ed. John T. McNeill, trans. Ford Lewis Battles [Philadelphia: Westminster, 1960], 3.10.6, page 725.
6. Mather, C. 2010. *A Christian at His Calling: Two Brief Discourses.* Gale ECCO Print Editions.

Notes

CHAPTER 9

It's Not All About Work

**CORRECTING HERESY #7:
"MEANINGFULNESS IS FOUND AT WORK."**

As Jeff neared his mission release date, he had a foreboding feeling. His time in Japan had been the most purposeful experience he could imagine. Now, an uncertain future was racing toward him. He recalls:

> I suddenly had to start thinking about **my** schooling, **my** finances, **my** career. Not only was I unnerved about all the important decisions that lay ahead of me, I also felt like I was entering a vacuum of purposelessness. How could thinking about myself ever give me the deep sense of consecration and purpose that a mission did? It was almost as if I was mourning the loss of my mission before it was even over.
>
> About this time, I attended one of my last zone conferences. As was his custom, my mission president ended the conference with an extended Q&A period, during which we missionaries could ask him anything we wanted. This seemed like the ideal opportunity to get some advice. So, I raised my hand and asked, "After our missions are over and we are no longer full-time servants of God, how can we keep a sense of purpose?" My mission president began to respond. But at that moment, his wife stood up next to him, and literally elbowed him aside. She said, "I'll take this one."

I still vividly remember her response. It was one of the most inspired pieces of counsel I have received. Her message went something like this: "When I do the laundry, I am building the kingdom of God. When I scrub the floors, I am serving the Lord. When I tidy the clutter, I'm an instrument in His hands. I do a lot of mundane jobs, but if my eye is single to God and I'm trying to serve my family, then I can feel as much purpose in my work as a missionary can."

To the soon-to-return missionary that I was, this message was a revelation: What we do is not as important as the spirit in which we do it. I had embraced the idea that being a missionary was the noblest of all pursuits. Perhaps I had even become a little prideful in that belief. Doing anything else seemed like a step down—a demotion—from the eternally significant responsibility of preaching the gospel. My mission president's wife reminded me that none of us, regardless of our title, has cornered the market on meaningfulness.

You hear a lot of folk wisdom that urges you to appreciate the opportunities you have been given: "Bloom where you are planted." "Make the most of what you are given." But what Jeff's mission president's wife taught him was more than about just being happy where you are. She wasn't just saying "be content in your station." Her unique message was that even mundane tasks can be absolutely drenched in meaningfulness if you are doing them for a worthy cause. And if there is one thing our research has taught us, it is that we human beings crave a sense of purpose. Yes, we like to enjoy ourselves. But even more than that, we want to *matter*. We will put up with very unpleasant tasks—maybe even smile through them—if we know they are for an important cause. One of the zookeepers we studied put it nicely when he said, "The thing about this job is anything I do is ultimately for the animals, even if it's scrubbing down the back hallways." Give us a strong sense of purpose, and we will usually pour our hearts into the most menial of chores.

The idea that a sense of purpose can make meaningful what otherwise is mundane and miserable was a core message in the work of the renowned psychologist Victor Frankl. Frankl knew something about misery. During World War II, he spent nearly three years imprisoned by the Nazis in Theresienstadt, Auschwitz, and Dachau. His wife, mother, and brother died in Nazi concentration camps. In the midst of his despair, Frankl discovered a sublime truth that became the central focus of his life and of his life's work. His discovery was this: we can endure and even thrive in any condition when we have a sense of purpose that is anchored in love for, and service to, others. He describes the power of that insight in the following experience from his Nazi imprisonment:

> *We stumbled on in the darkness, over big stones and through large puddles, along the one road leading from the camp. The accompanying guards kept shouting at us and driving us with the butts of their rifles. Anyone with very sore feet supported himself on his neighbor's arm. Hardly a word was spoken; the icy wind did not encourage talk. Hiding his mouth behind his upturned collar, the man marching next to me whispered suddenly: "If our wives could see us now! I do hope they are better off in their camps and don't know what is happening to us."*
>
> *That brought thoughts of my own wife to mind... [M]y mind clung to my wife's image, imagining it with an uncanny acuteness. I heard her answering me, saw her smile, her frank and encouraging look. Real or not, her look was then more luminous than the sun which was beginning to rise.*
>
> *A thought transfixed me: for the first time in my life I saw the truth as it is set into song by so many poets, proclaimed as the final wisdom by so many thinkers. The truth—that love is the ultimate and the highest goal to which Man can aspire. Then I*

grasped the meaning of the greatest secret that human poetry and human thought and belief have to impart: The salvation of Man is through love and in love. I understood how a man who has nothing left in this world still may know bliss, be it only for a brief moment, in the contemplation of his beloved. In a position of utter desolation, when Man cannot express himself in positive action, when his only achievement may consist in enduring his sufferings in the right way—an honorable way—in such a position Man can, through loving contemplation of the image he carries of his beloved, achieve fulfillment. For the first time in my life I was able to understand the meaning of the words, "The angels are lost in perpetual contemplation of an infinite glory."

Frankl often summarized this insight with the following quote by Friedrich Nietzsche: "He who has a strong enough why can bear almost any how."

Based on his experiences, Frankly developed a stream of psychotherapy called "logotherapy"—psychological healing through meaning.

You will probably not be called upon to face anything like Frankl experienced. But purpose is still vitally important in your personal and professional life.

Choosing a "Dissertation" in Life

Asking yourself big questions about finding a life purpose can be daunting. Financial worries and personal insecurities might convince you that pursuing a higher purpose is a luxury you can't afford, or can't achieve. Jeff recalls confronting these doubts in his mid-twenties:

Having been raised in a home where my parents struggled to make ends meet, I had convinced myself that the most important thing was to find a job that would help me live comfortably. I tried to suppress any idealistic feelings I had about my career, and started exploring ways to get the highest-paying job I could find. I enrolled in the MBA program at BYU with that goal in mind.

During MBA orientation, a general authority came to speak to us to welcome us into the program. I was excited to receive an inspiring message from one of the Lord's servants. But the talk turned out to be the worst talk I had ever heard from a general authority—at least, so I told myself at the time. The speaker was a newly called member of the Quorum of the Seventy, a man I hadn't heard of (named Henry B. Eyring!). I don't have a transcript of his talk, so I can't represent accurately the fullness of his message. But one major theme was impossible for me to forget. As I recall, he taught along the following lines: "You may not be planning to get a PhD, but I challenge each of you to choose a 'dissertation in life' nonetheless. Find a problem that you will become a world-class expert on. Find a cause that you can devote your career to, and that will bless the world and Heavenly Father's children."

That was not what I wanted to hear! In fact, I remember leaving that talk feeling angry, and telling myself I would simply forget a message that was so impractical and frustratingly lofty. After all, I had decided to just be a good businessperson and make as much money as I could.

*Well, of course, I didn't forget that message. It haunted me as the days, weeks, and months of my MBA program passed. I came to realize that then-Elder Eyring's message was the most important thing I could hear right then. By choosing to make money for its own sake, I was simply trying to run away from what my heart was telling me—that I **had** to work for a cause. I was rationalizing my money-making motives because I was afraid to do the hard work of figuring out what my dissertation in life should be.*

It was many more years later before Jeff fully realized that Elder Eyring had also provided him with an important hint about how to *find* his calling. Jeff had spent so much time trying to figure out what would make *him* happy that he had given almost no thought to what he could do to make *others* happy. Ironically, the way you come to understand your gifts is by giving them, not by analyzing and numerating them. It is only in the giving that you can figure out *your* way to give.

There is a story, perhaps apocryphal, that helps to teach this principle. It is said that Christopher Wren, the brilliant architect of Saint Paul's Cathedral in London, approached a workman chipping away at some stone during the construction of the church. Wren asked the man what he was doing. He responded, "I'm just laying bricks." The architect walked over to another laborer and posed the same question. The second man responded, "Can you not see? I am building a great cathedral to God!" These two men were doing identical tasks. But the meaning they assigned to their work was worlds apart. Only the man who viewed his work as an offering experienced the joy of a calling.

Forgetting about Passion?

The seventh and final heresy is that meaning in life is to be found at work. This heresy is particularly tantalizing because it is partly true. Your work *can* give you a keen sense of purpose and importance. Recognition, promotions, and work successes boost your ego and help you see why you matter. But the seventh heresy misses the mark—and ultimately leaves you feeling empty—because it gets things all backwards.

If you hear someone say, "I want to do work that gives me a sense of purpose," then you should stop and notice the pronouns she is using. Seeking personal meaning through work tends to focus you on "I" and "me." And the Savior had very pointed things to say about the trap of self-gratification. Of all His teachings, one of the most paradoxical is: "For whosoever will save his life shall lose it: and whosoever will lose his life for my sake shall find it" (Matthew 16:25). Here is one of the grand ironies of life! If you put self-gratification first, it becomes a mirage you can never catch up with. But when you lose yourself in good causes (and specifically, for the Savior's sake), suddenly there it is: the deep satisfaction that can't be found by looking for it.

So, there is a danger in going on a personal quest for meaningfulness in your career, especially if you do it without regard for others. You can lose sight of your best gifts when all of your focus is on personal advancement. You could find yourself in the tragic but all-too-common state of worldly renown but internal emptiness. The Savior's teaching surely applies to your work life as well. You can only really find your calling by losing yourself "for His sake"—and working for His sake means working for God's children. Meaningful work isn't something you can find by looking for it. You have to *give* your way into meaningful work.

And this is not just a religious argument. David Brooks, a columnist for the New York Times, drove the point home in an article. Today's college graduates, he said,

> *"...are sent off into this world with the whole baby-boomer theology ringing in their ears. If you sample some of the commencement addresses being broadcast on C-Span these days, you see that many graduates are told to: Follow your passion, chart your own course, march to the beat of your own drummer, follow your dreams and find yourself. This is the litany of expressive individualism, which is still the dominant note in American culture...*

"Most successful young people don't look inside and then plan a life. They look outside and find a problem, which summons their life. A relative suffers from Alzheimer's and a young woman feels called to help cure that disease. A young man works under a miserable boss, and must develop management skills so his department can function. Another young woman finds herself confronted by an opportunity she never thought of in a job category she never imagined. This wasn't in her plans, but this is where she can make her contribution.

"Most people don't form a self and then lead a life. They are called by a problem, and the self is constructed gradually by their calling."[1]

Called by a problem! This is a very different way to shape your career than focusing on self-gratification, money, or fun. What looks "fun" to you when you are young might end up feeling empty when you are older. In fact, seasoned people are more likely to tell you that what's "fun" is leaving a legacy, making a difference, giving back. But that kind of fun is really hard work. It involves paying dues, enduring drudgery, and encountering baffling setbacks. Being "called by a problem" means that you may grapple with that problem for years, and sometimes feel bested by it. But even when things aren't going too well, you can still experience a sense of focus and direction that keeps you moving forward and engaged in your work.

This principle should ring true for those who have chosen to raise children rather than pursue a career. Mothers are, in a sense, "called by a problem"—the problem of bringing up a posterity that is responsible, faithful, loved and loving. Motherhood is a monumental service. And it allows women to bring their unique spiritual gifts and gradually discover *their* way of being a great mother.

Another columnist, Oliver Segovia (from the Harvard Business School) put it starkly by titling an essay, "To Find Happiness, Forget About Passion."[2] When we first saw that title, our gut reaction was "Oh, this is wrong!" But Segovia actually gets it absolutely right. He argues that the key to happiness *isn't* prioritizing your own dreams, but rather finding a need that you can fill. His thesis is that you are getting it backwards when you put passion before service. Passion for its own sake turns out to be hollow. If, however, you put your passion *into* service... well, that's sustainable passion, and a recipe for professional happiness.

Lessons from the Bear Whisperer

One of our favorite examples of someone putting his passion into service is Steve Searles, who is best known as "The Bear Whisperer." That's also the title of the reality television program that he stars in on Animal Planet. Steve's story is remarkable because his job didn't even exist until he saw a problem that his gifts would allow him to solve.

Jeff met up with Steve at a coffee shop in Mammoth Lakes, California in the middle of a blizzard on a Saturday morning. Steve generously shared his time (not typical celebrity behavior) to tell his story. He put on no airs. In fact, he struck Jeff as a true outdoorsman—grizzled beard, earthy language, and clearly less comfortable around people than he would have been out in the mountains. But he also had an intense, earnest kindness about him. He spoke as articulately and intelligently as any scholar you might meet.

Thirty-five years ago, the city of Mammoth Lakes hired Steve, a young, avid, amateur animal tracker, to solve a bear problem. The growing bear population was frightening visitors and interfering with the tourism industry. The city gave Steve a "hit list" of bears to kill.

But Steve had been observing the local bears carefully for years, and he had discerned some remarkable things about their behavior. He had noticed, for instance, that the local bears maintained an orderly hierarchy. The bears with the most status exhibited dominant behaviors—assertive posture, loud vocal signals—toward the bears with lower status. Bears that expressed these behaviors were able to exert their will over others and keep them in line. Steve wondered if he might be able to use the bears' own status system to manage them and keep them out of trouble in town. At any rate, he was hoping to find a better solution than exterminating the local bear population.

Steve asked the city manager if he could try "educating" the bears rather than killing them. The city manager thought this was ludicrous. You can't train bears in the wild! But Steve was persuasive. His employer finally agreed to give him a few months to try out his ideas, but he was pessimistic that it would work. Thus began Steve's grand experiment: to try to turn himself into the biggest, baddest bear in town so that the real bears would know their place.

Steve began adopting the bears' status-asserting postures and mimicking their vocal signals when he encountered them. He experimented with pellet guns and pyrotechnics to show the bears that when they were in town, they were on *his* turf and had better behave. Gradually, the bears came to recognize Steve, and exhibit deferential behavior toward him when they were in town. Incidents of bears damaging property began to decline.

However, Steve also wanted the bears to understand that they were entitled to their freedom when they were in the forest. So Steve changed his behavior entirely when he was in the woods with the bears. There, he stayed silent and displayed submissive postures. Gradually, the bears seemed to grasp where their place was, and what the boundaries were. They have come to recognize Steve when they see him. They even allow him to visit their dens and play with their cubs!

Steve's innovative approach to bear management succeeded even beyond his hopes. One of the most surprising results was that the bears started to "police" themselves. They train their young to respect Steve's boundaries, and chase off intruding bears who don't follow Steve's rules. They have not only learned the rules; they enforce them.

Mammoth Lakes is now widely regarded as the worldwide model for the coexistence of bears and humans. In addition to becoming a television celebrity, Steve now trains other communities with bear populations to implement his techniques.

After 35 years in his "bear whisperer" career, how many bears has Steve had to kill because of aggressive behavior? You guessed it. Zero.

It's important to note that when Steve first started sharing his techniques with others, the scholarly community mocked him. They didn't believe bears could respond to emotions like respect and love, which were the central features of Steve's theory of bear behavior. Steve often felt rejected by the community that most needed his gifts. Developing his calling was a difficult path, full of obstacles and challenges. But Steve felt driven by his cause. He loved his bears so much that he would gladly confront adversity in order to serve them.

Today, Steve's astonishing results are changing people's minds about social relationships among bears. In any case, there is no denying that Steve has saved the lives of countless bears. He has also boosted the tourism industry in Mammoth Lakes because of the possibility of viewing wild bears in safety. To put it differently, by following his passions and his instincts, Steve has literally created a new profession, perfectly suited to his gifts, and beautifully aligned with a cause he believes in. How's that for a calling in life!

Notice, though, that Steve didn't set out to follow *his* passions. He was compelled by a cause that was as unique as his gifts. He was willing to confront the risk of physical harm, social mockery, and failure because he cared so much about the well-being of bears. His cause is what led him to his calling. In fact, when Steve steps back and looks at where his career has taken him, he is astonished. He never aspired to become a celebrity with his own TV show. In fact, if that *had* been his aspiration, it seems almost certain that he would have failed.

Like most of the zookeepers we studied, Steve attributes his professional success to luck. During our conversation, he said:

> *"You'll never find someone as lucky as me in your interviews. They gave me a task [to manage the bear population], and I just looked for the easiest solution. Life just came by and tapped me on my shoulder."*

Steve might call it luck, but we believe that it is something more. Many people we have interviewed have said that they were lucky to find their calling. But these "lucky" people all seem to have something in common: They pour their hearts into a problem, using their unique gifts to solve it. When you use your spiritual gifts to serve, Heavenly Father opens doors, whether you recognize His hand or not.

To conclude Steve's story, here is how he feels about his work:

"It's not just my job; it's my hobby. It's my pastime. I haven't gone on vacation in ten years. I live in a postcard! I work with wild animals every day. I love every friggin' day. I can't get to work fast enough in the morning."

The Touch of Service

Remarkable stories like the Bear Whisperer's might seem overwhelming if you haven't figured out what you want to contribute to the world. You might be saying, "Hey, I'm *willing* to serve other people at work, but I have no idea how to do it. What could *I* possibly give? I'm just an average person." But remember, Steve didn't set out to be a television star; he just poured himself into solving a problem and the rest followed.

We told the story of Dr. Dale Hull in an earlier chapter. As you will recall, a horrific trampoline accident stole from him what he thought was his calling: delivering babies. As he shared his recovery story, he said something that really struck us to the heart. Immediately after his accident, Dale had no movement in his body below the neck. He had to rely entirely upon nurses to care for his every physical need. That was very humbling for him. In addition, he had no feeling anywhere except for his face. So the only physical contact he could register was when the nurses washed his face. Dale said, with obvious emotion, that when the nurses wiped his face, he could tell merely from their touch whether they were giving care, or just doing a job. The simplest contact, in the only way Dale could receive it, revealed to him the inner motivations of his nurses.

You have probably heard the story, "The Touch of the Master's Hand," in which a brilliant violinist reveals the value of a beat-up instrument by playing it masterfully. But there is also a "touch of the servant's hand," which is what Dale experienced. Even if you aren't brilliant or talented, your simple offerings of service to others are the sacred touch of the servant's hand. You can't fake the touch of service, anymore than you could fake being a talented violinist. You might sometimes be ham-handed or awkward in what you do. But when you serve with compassion, caring and selflessness, the authenticity registers, and your work becomes an offering.

Jeff gained a deeper appreciation for the touch of service from Santiago Michalek, the artist we mentioned earlier in the book. After getting to know Santiago and falling in love with his work, Jeff decided to commission him to paint a portrait of his son, depicting their experience together in Ghana. Here are Jeff's reflections:

That trip with my son had been extremely meaningful to me because of the unique memories we made together. In particular, I wanted this painting to capture the memory of my son interacting with children at an orphanage. I knew that Santiago was the artist to do it.

Having never commissioned a painting before, I didn't know what to expect. I thought that I would hand over a photograph and Santiago would simply reproduce it in oil. But the process of working with Santiago as he created the portrait turned out to be far more emotional than I could have imagined. Santiago spent a lot of time talking with me before he ever put brush to canvas. He asked me to talk to him about what my son means to me, about what the experience of being in Africa meant for our relationship, and about my motives for commissioning the work. I explained that our Ghana trip was one of my best memories with my son, and that it had been hard on me to see him grow distant from me as he explores his independence. I told him that my motivation was to "freeze" that moment so that I would always have it.

After we talked, Santiago felt dissatisfied with the photos I had given him. None of them allowed him to express what I had described. So he called my son in to model for him, and took hundreds of photos, searching for the right expression that he could integrate into the photos I had provided.

When I saw Santiago's completed painting for the first time, I was surprised. It wasn't the painting I had envisioned, but instead it was something far more artistic. The expression on my son's face wasn't a sentimental snapshot image of him beaming down on an African child (which is what I, a non-artist, would have done). Instead, my son is looking directly out from the canvas, as if to invite you into the moment when he hands a soccer ball to the children clustering around him. The look on his face is an understated half-smile, as if his attention was momentarily drawn away from the children. It looked exactly like my son, the expression natural and authentic. But my first thought was, "shouldn't he be beaming with joy?"

I didn't verbalize that thought, but Santiago seemed instinctively to understand what I was trying to process in my mind. He said, as near as I recall:

"Let me tell you what was happening when I took the photo that I used for this painting. I was having a hard time getting your son to relax and look natural as he was modeling for me. So I just started asking him what it was like to go to Ghana with his Dad. He started talking then, and told me how cool it was to have a memory like that with his father. At that moment, he seemed to relax, and got this very reflective, nostalgic, grateful look on his *face. I snapped a picture in that moment, and that's the picture I used.*

"As I was painting this portrait, I kept thinking about your relationship with your son, and how hard it is to have a son grow up and separate himself from his parents. But in that moment in my studio, what I saw on you son's face was: 'I'm still here, Dad. I'm still your son.'"

At those words, I began to weep. I left with a treasure that is much more than a pretty picture. Far beyond simply painting a portrait, Santiago had delved deeply into my emotions, and also into my son's. He devoted many hours of work (most of it focused on painting my son's face) to ensure that he captured not only his likeness, but also his character. The result is a representation that is true physically, but also emotionally. When I look at this piece, I see my son's spirit looking back at me.

*Santiago didn't just do a job for me. He served me. He also taught me that a calling goes far beyond talent and effort. There is a spiritual dimension to a calling. It's not just about the **hand** and the **mind**—the typical instruments of work. It also includes a heavy dose of **heart** and **spirit**. I want to be a true artist like he is, not in the same medium, but with the same level of consecrated devotion to others.*

Shortly after his experience with Santiago, Jeff was struck once again by this principle, but in another setting. (Isn't it remarkable how the Lord drives home important lessons repeatedly in a short amount of time?) Jeff had recently begun taking voice lessons—something he had always wished to do, but had postponed for years because of insecurity and self-doubt. But his teacher assured him that he would be able to learn to sing. He recalls one lesson:

My teacher was always trying to convince me that my voice has natural beauty. I found that tough to swallow. But then during one of our lessons, in the middle of some soft legato exercises, she stopped me and said the following (reproduced verbatim from my audio recording of the session):

"OK, here's something to think about, because I know that this whole idea of your voice being beautiful is foreign to you and kind of embarrasses you a little bit... Um, instead of thinking about your voice, think about what your voice is doing **to** someone.

If you could hug someone with your voice... if you could envelop someone with warmth and love, instead of 'oh, it's about my voice.' To give! To give to somebody else. Does that make sense?"

It certainly did make sense. It went straight to my heart. And when I started thinking about singing to express love for someone, the energy changed, my focus changed, and things flowed much more naturally. Maybe even a little bit—dare I say it?—beautifully.

Stuart had an experience with a fellow church member that reinforced this same principle, but in a different context. The member confided to him, with some embarrassment and hesitation, that she was struggling to find joy in her temple service. She had always heard that temple attendance should be a sublime spiritual experience. But instead of fulfillment, she felt anxious, uncomfortable, and distracted at the temple.

As he talked to her, Stuart encouraged this sister to remember that temple service is, first and foremost, service. We don't go to the temple for personal gratification, but rather for what we can give as "saviors on Mount Zion."

A month after this conversation, Stuart ran into this sister again. She told him that she had started thinking about temple attendance as service. The change in perspective had made all the difference. She couldn't wait to get back to the temple, and expressed a newfound love for temple service. It's amazing what comes back to you when you lose yourself in service to others.

The touch of service means that you approach your work as a giver. You aren't there to prove how smart, talented, or effective you are. You aren't there primarily for our own welfare. You are there to give your very best to people who need you, whether your impact is direct or indirect. It's impossible to find a calling in any other way. Until you are offering service to others, you are just doing a job. But when service is the core of your work, you find your calling and offer the world something beautiful.

But there is one final way that the seventh heresy gets it all wrong. And it's another grand irony.

The Motivational Power of Giving

A core doctrine of economic theory is that humans are self-interested creatures. If you want to get people to work harder, offer them a financial reward. Our very economic system is based on this doctrine. Recent research, however, is challenging the belief that people are fundamentally selfish beings. Multiple studies are telling us, loud and clear, that we humans are a lot more motivated when we are working for other people than if we are working for ourselves.

Now, it's true that most people do feel motivated to earn money—but only up to a point and within specific limits. You might work very hard to reach a subsistence level of income. But after you reach that stage, it turns out that money doesn't have as much motivational oomph as you might think. To get to truly peak levels of motivation, people need to feel they are helping others. The human race might just be more wired for service than for selfishness.

The author Daniel Pink engagingly describes many new research findings about motivation in his book, *Drive*. Together, these studies illustrate how financial rewards can actually undermine your performance, and make you less creative. Conversely, he shows that having a sense of purpose accounts for some of the greatest innovations of our day. Take Wikipedia, for instance. It's easily the world's most successful encyclopedia, but it is composed and maintained almost entirely by highly knowledgeable *volunteer* experts (and, granted, more than a few hacks). They get zero compensation, and little credit, for their contributions.

Why are some of the smartest people in the world willing to give away their expertise for free, even while sacrificing countless hours to make sure Wikipedia is accurate? Pink argues that it's because the feeling of contributing to something important is inherently motivational. Giving ignites your imagination, he argues, and propels you to do better work than you would otherwise.

The reason that giving is motivational is a little surprising: Rendering service changes *you*.

Our good friend and colleague, Adam Grant (a professor at the Wharton School of Business), has made a career of showing how "pro-social motivation" transforms people at work. One of our favorite of Adam's studies was an experiment he did with telefund employees. These are the college students who call alums on the phone to ask for donations. It's tedious, frustrating work. Students quickly get burned out after being turned down over and over again on the phone. Employee turnover at telefunds is extremely high. But Adam thought he could influence telefund employees' motivation by tweaking one little thing: he invited some of the employees to have a five-minute conversation with a student who had received scholarship money from the telefund's efforts.

The result? It's actually a little hard to believe. Not only did employees start placing considerably more phone calls after their conversation with the scholarship recipient. But they also posted a *400% increase* in donations they solicited. In other words, interacting with a real person who benefited from their work made the employees *far* more effective at asking for donations.

But the effect only lasted for a day or two, right? Wrong. Employees who had interacted with a scholarship recipient were still performing at much higher levels two months later. There are very few motivational techniques that work like magic. But Dr. Grant and other researchers are showing that helping people is magical. When you personally connect with the people who benefit from your work, you pour your heart into it much more than if you were just trying to make a buck.

In fact, we submit that you don't really have a calling until you can point to someone or something you are serving. *Service* is an essential—almost definitional—part of the deep satisfaction that we long for in our jobs. A podiatrist friend articulated it very well:

> *"Thinking of my own calling, I think I'm lucky enough to have found it. But even so, it's not like I wake up every day excited to go to work. Looking at feet, after all, is not a very glorious job. But what makes my job great is helping so many people to feel better. It's the service aspect that really makes my job great. While I'm working to help the patients that come to see me, I never think of myself or my own problems or worry about how much money I'm making."*

And that's the lesson that the Savior taught. Your work will be satisfying and meaningful when you lose yourself (and your financial preoccupations) in serving others. On the other hand, you can spend your career hungrily seeking gratification and never find it, nor leave a lasting mark. As Phillip Brooks, noted clergyman of the late 1800s, reportedly observed: "How carefully most men creep into nameless graves, while now and again one or two forget themselves into immortality." You have to forget yourself into your calling in life.

What To Do Now

1. In your journal, reflect on jobs you have held in the past. What service did you render in them? Whom did you help? Reflect on how opportunities to serve impacted your feelings about your work.

2. Develop a list of the ways that your current work (or the work you might someday do) can assist in building the Kingdom of God. Who will benefit directly from your work? Who will benefit indirectly?

3. Create an opportunity to have a conversation with a few people who benefit from the work you do now. Ask them what you can do to better serve them. Find out how your work contributes to what they need.

4. Consider devoting a fast to asking the Lord to help you understand how you can best serve Him professionally. Pray intently to ask where and how you can use your unique spiritual gifts to be of service to others. Follow the principles taught by Elder Scott in April 2012 General Conference as you seek personal revelation about what you should do at work to exercise greater discipleship.

Endnotes

1. Brooks, D. 2011. It's Not About You. *New York Times*, May 30.
2. Harvard Business Review Blog Network. See: http://blogs.hbr.org/cs/2012/01/to_find_happiness_forget_about.html

Notes

Notes

CHAPTER 10

Mapping Out Your Life's Work: An Exercise

The nine previous chapters show how the doctrines of the world inhibit you from finding your life calling. But we hope you have gained more than just warnings. If you have followed along with the activities in this book, then you have already done some important work. In this final chapter, we will help you pull together what you have learned by leading you through a final exercise. It will result in a personalized diagram of your calling in life as you understand it now. But before we launch into the exercise, let's pause for some perspective.

Putting Work into Perspective

Several years ago, Stuart spoke with a church leader about career concerns. The wise leader listened thoughtfully. He then said: "I think that someday, with the benefit of an eternal perspective, we will look back on our careers and realize that we were like children playing with blocks. We will find that what we thought was so important was really very small and insignificant when it comes to the things that really matter." The church leader then proceeded to extend Stuart a Church calling.

In writing this book, we have been keenly conscious of a challenging irony. It is this: On the one hand, the work you choose to do in this life is vitally important because it shapes who you become and who you serve. On the other hand, the work you choose to do in this life is virtually immaterial; no matter your job or role, your primary identity is "child of God," and you can serve Him and His children no matter what sort of work you do.

So which is it? Which position is truest in an eternal perspective? Paradoxically, we argue in the next two sections that *both* are true.

The Work You Do Doesn't Matter

Unless you choose a career that is fundamentally dishonest or corrupt, your job choice will have no bearing on your admission into the Celestial Kingdom. The blessings of the priesthood are fully accessible to any worthy person, regardless of job title. So as you ponder, fret, and agonize about your career choices, it's important to recognize that your eternal happiness is not at stake.

In the April 2012 General Conference, Pres. Dieter F. Uchtdorf spoke about regrets. He suggested that "perhaps the most universal regret" that people face at the end of their lives is a wish that they had spent less time at work, and more time with the people they loved. He cited work by palliative nurse and author Bronnie Ware (from her book *The Top Five Regrets of the Dying*), who said that every single dying man she interviewed expressed regret for "spending so much of their lives on the treadmill of a work existence."[1] This should remind us of the tortured, chain-ridden ghost Jacob Marley in Charles Dickens' *A Christmas Carol*, who warned his business partner Ebenezer Scrooge: "In life, my spirit never rose beyond the limits of our money-changing holes! Now I am doomed to wander without rest or peace, incessant torture and remorse!"

Clearly, when you face your final moments of life, the jobs you did here on earth will *not* be your most important work. Your most important callings in life are spouse, parent, child, sibling, friend, and disciple.

The Work You Do Matters a Great Deal

So why should you bother searching for a calling in life? Why not set aside ambition and interests, and just focus on building a strong home? There are at least a couple of reasons why a disciple *should* strive for meaningful work.

First, you will probably spend a huge portion of your waking life doing work. Some people just mark time at work to feed their families. There is no indignity in that. But there may not be much progress either. If you turn off your heart and brain for eight, nine, or ten hours per day, you may be squandering time when the Lord can use you to bless His children through your work.

Secondly, as we discussed in Chapter 6, if your work is just a spirit-sapping drudgery, then you will have less to give your family and friends when you get home from work. We humans aren't meant to turn on and off like light bulbs. It's very difficult to spend a day at work doing things that benumb you, and then come home and vibrantly love those who matter most.

So, although work is *not* the purpose of life, finding meaningful work *does* matter for a follower of Christ. Work should be an arena that refines you, that increases your capacity to do good things. Work should give you an outlet to serve Heavenly Father's children. Finding a calling in life is not necessary for salvation. But serving others is. If you root your work in service, you increase your capacity to become a saint because you discover more about your gifts and you directly involve yourself in God's work to bless His children.

Mapping Your Calling in Life

With those two seemingly contradictory (but equally true) principles in mind, let's begin the exercise. It's critical that you work along with each step we describe, taking time to reflect upon and answer the questions we pose. Simply reading the chapter won't provide you much personal insight.

Another "ground rule" for this exercise is that you write in pencil (figuratively, if not literally). The diagram you draw may look very different a few years from now after you have gained more life experiences and spiritual promptings. So consider this exercise a tentative attempt to identify your calling, recognizing that your understanding will develop and deepen over time. Don't worry too much about "getting it right."

Your diagram—we call it a "calling map"—will comprise three pieces, each of which will appear as circles (of varying sizes, and varying levels of overlap). The three circles are based on our research findings, and have deep roots in the restored gospel. For the sake of simplicity, we will use worldly terminology for them: Passion, Place and Purpose. (We like alliteration.) But we will also point out the doctrinal bases of each concept and invite you to approach this exercise prayerfully, seeking inspiration as you consider how you want your work to contribute to the world.

As we describe each of the three components, think about their relative importance for *you* personally. Some circles are bound to be more prominent in your calling map than others.

Passion

As we described in Chapter 2, one of the defining features of a life calling is "hardwiring"—a feeling that you are naturally predisposed to do some things and not others. For zookeepers, hardwiring meant that they knew at a young age that they were meant to work with animals. They were born "animal people." Hardwiring creates a sense of *passion*—an intense desire to pursue a particular activity or interest.

Hardwiring is all about spiritual gifts, which are sometimes very pronounced, even at a young age. Consider the example of Kevin.

Mapping Out Your Life's Work: An Exercise

Almost from infancy, mechanical things fascinated him: He loved taking things apart; He had a knack for seeing how things could fit together; He absolutely loved cars. People who know Kevin tend to say, "he was born to be a mechanic." His highly specialized spiritual gifts led him to a passion he enjoys for automotive engineering.

Whether or not you have developed a clear understanding of your spiritual gifts, the point we'd like to make is that some people are more driven by passion than are others. This is simply an individual difference, and not a matter of right and wrong. So, how important is passion to you?

In a few pages, we will ask you to represent your sense of passion by drawing a circle. If you have always known what type of work you want to do, then you will make your passion circle large. (Kevin's passion circle would be very large indeed.) If, however, you don't feel a strong drive toward particular activities, your circle will be smaller. But before you start drawing this circle, let's look at the other circles that will make up your map.

Purpose

Some people feel drawn to a cause; they want to meet someone's needs or solve a particular problem. They might not even care *how* they contribute to it, as long as they can be involved. A good example is a friend we'll call Sally. Sally came from a broken home, which had been devastated by her father's pornography addiction. Imagine her horror when several years into her marriage, her husband admitted to her that he, too, was addicted to pornography. Determined to spare her own family the agony she felt as a child, Sally began studying addiction recovery and working with her husband, who also was highly committed to overcoming his challenges. As the years passed, there was more success than failure (though some of both), and Sally discovered that the principles of addiction recovery had strengthened her marriage and given her a keen sense of purpose. Sally has become involved in the addiction recovery cause both as a professional and as a volunteer. Although she has many talents to offer, she cares less about what she does as long as she remains involved in the cause.

Sally, and people like her, have a stronger sense of "purpose" than "passion." To clarify the difference, passion is something *inside* of you—a spiritual gift or talent you feel compelled to express (like Kevin's mechanical skill). Purpose, on the other hand, is something *outside* of you—a cause that beckons you to help. It should remind you of the verse in D&C 59 we referred to earlier that instructs people to be "anxiously engaged in a good cause... of their own free will."

Some people feel so much synergy between their passion and their purpose that they can't separate them. Our zookeeper friends, for instance, felt that their passion for animal care was completely enmeshed in the cause of wildlife conservation. A gifted singer might feel that her passion for singing is identical to her love for uplifting an audience. But these really are two separate things. Passion represents the spiritual gifts that are within us. Purpose represents a cause outside of us that compels us to serve. It's wonderful when these two things overlap, but they don't always (as we'll see soon).

How important is purpose to you? If you want to be part of a cause, to join together with other people to solve a particular problem or to serve society in some way, then you should draw a large "purpose" circle in your calling map. But there is one more element to consider first.

Place

The third element of calling is a sense of place—a feeling that you are where you are supposed to be, whether you know *why* you are there or not. As you might recall from Chapter 2, our zookeeper friends felt that the hand of fate had led them to where they were supposed to be.

Even though none of them spoke explicitly about God, they sensed that a higher power had guided them.

If you have a strong sense of place, it means that you feel drawn—spiritually and emotionally—to a particular location or setting. One former student provides a good example. Jose grew up in a mid-sized city in the Midwest, a city facing economic stagnation and serious social problems. Jose was an extremely bright business school student, so he had many lucrative career opportunities to choose from. But Jose felt an irresistible pull back to his roots. He decided to pursue a public service career working for the city. He dreamed of becoming mayor. Jose's calling in life didn't relate so much to specific talents or causes (he wasn't sure yet what problem he should tackle, or how). But he knew precisely *where* he wanted to be.

Place is core to your calling if you yearn to work for a particular organization or a specific profession—or if you feel drawn to devote your life to homemaking. It might also be a geographical tug, as it was for Jose.

Do you feel like the Lord is drawing you to a particular place or profession? Have you received strong assurances about where you are supposed to be? If so, then you will draw a large circle to represent your sense of place.

Now, let's get to work.

STEP I: Size Your Circles

Now that we have described passion, purpose, and place, it's your turn to make sense of what they mean in your life. Think carefully about how important these three elements are *to you*. There are no right or wrong answers. Nor are you making a lifetime commitment as you begin to sketch your calling map.

To help you decide how big each of your three circles will be, consider the following points and questions:

Passion is about *what* and *how:*

- Have you always had a strong sense of *what activities* you want to do as your life's work?
- Do you have a clear sense of what your unique gifts and talents are? Will these affect *what* you choose to do and *how* you do it?

Purpose is about *why:*

- Do you have a strong desire to pursue a particular cause or solve a particular problem?
- Do you think a lot about *why* you would do a particular kind of work?

Place is about *where:*

- Do you feel drawn to a particular organization, industry or geographic location? Do you know *where* you want to be?
- Do you have a strong sense that the Lord has led you to be *where* you are today, even if you don't yet know why?

The stronger your "yes" answers are to any of these questions, the larger you should draw that particular circle. Here are a couple of examples to show you what this might look like:

PASSION **PURPOSE** **PLACE**

The circles above might have been drawn by one of the zookeepers that we studied. She would tell you that she is driven by a specific passion: caring for animals. So her passion circle is the largest. Her purpose (species preservation) also matters, but doesn't motivate her quite

Mapping Out Your Life's Work: An Exercise

as strongly as working with animals. So the purpose circle is a little smaller. Finally, this zookeeper doesn't feel a strong need to identify with a particular place. She could see herself pursuing her passion at other zoos, or even in another profession, such as veterinary medicine.

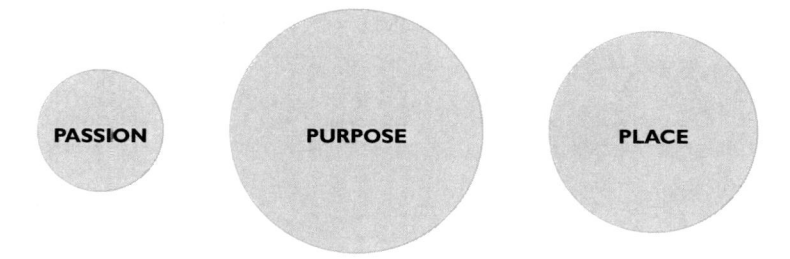

PASSION   **PURPOSE**   **PLACE**

The next set of circles (above) are typical of those who feel called to military service. They tend to have a very keen sense of purpose: defending the freedom of the United States of America. Most, too, have a very strong sense of place; they feel a bone-deep connection to their branch of the military. Passion often is less important for these people, however. They are willing to serve their country in any way that is needed. They welcome assignments that use their gifts, of course. But their calling does not depend on a perfect alignment with their unique talents.

Take some time now to draw your three circles, sizing them according to the weight you would give their importance in your own life. We recommend that you draw them at the top of a blank page of paper, leaving plenty of space beneath them so that you can add in material for the next step.

STEP 2: Fill in the Contents

This second step may be the most important. Now that you have drawn three empty circles, you should identify what's "inside" of them. If you have been thinking carefully about the questions we posed in previous chapters, then you should already have a lot of ideas about what passion, purpose, and place mean to you. But something magical happens when you write down your ideas. They become more concrete, and new ideas tend to follow rapidly. This is one of the reasons that journaling is such a powerful tool for self-discovery. Elder Richard G. Scott has taught that when we record spiritual impressions, the Lord multiplies them (see Elder Scott's April 2012 General Conference address).

So, in this step, you will jot down what passion, purpose, and place mean to you personally. Allow yourself to write freely. Don't pay attention to grammar or spelling. Don't even worry about writing in complete sentences. The important thing is to let the ideas flow and capture the relevant thoughts that come to your head.

Go back to the page with your three circles. Starting with the largest circle, write down (underneath it, or on a separate page) your ideas about what that circle means to you. Give yourself plenty of time and jot down everything that comes to mind. When you have exhausted your ideas for your largest circle, move on to your next largest one and do the same thing. Then end with your smallest circle.

To help you with this step of the exercise, we provide a list of thought-inducing questions below, one set each for passion, purpose, and place. Many of these questions are similar to ones we asked in earlier chapters. You don't have to answer all of them. Some will resonate with you, while others may not. But at least consider each of them and see what ideas they generate. List your ideas under the relevant circle as they occur to you.

We have provided (in Appendix 1 after this chapter) three examples of what this step looked like for people who completed the exercise. They include Jeff, Anna (a Chinese graduate student), and Wendy (an athletic administrator). Use these examples as references, but not as templates to copy. Notice, though, that each example is very specific. **Push *far* beyond trite phrases** such as "I like to help people." Instead, describe *how* you help, and *which* people, for instance. The more precise and specific you are, the more insights you will gain.

Passion Questions

- What are some of your unique gifts and talents?
- Think back on your childhood. What did you do for play? What do these activities tell you about your natural talents and interests?
- If someone offered you a free day to do any creative or productive activity you like, what would you choose to do?
- When have you found yourself "getting lost" in an activity? When do you feel you have done your very best work?
- What types of things do other people come to you to ask for help with?
- When you think back on your proudest moments, what were you doing?
- What combination of talents and abilities makes you unique?

Purpose Questions

- If someone offered you all the money you could ever need in exchange for devoting your life to a cause, what cause would you choose to pursue?
- What type of people are you most eager to help? What types of problems are you most eager to solve?
- Think back to the happiest times in your life. What were you working toward? What were you providing to others?
- What types of news stories catch your attention? What types of issues do you feel most drawn to learn about?
- When have you felt like you were part of something important and meaningful? What, exactly, inspired you during that time?

Place Questions

- Is there an organization or a setting that you feel drawn toward? Is there a place where you feel like you are supposed to be?
- Think about a time when you really felt like you belonged. What about your environment made it feel so right?
- Consider the places you have been in the past. How did you see the hand of the Lord leading you there? How have they prepared you for future opportunities and experiences?
- How settled do you feel where you are right now? Do you feel pulled in a different direction? If so, how would you describe the promptings you are receiving? What do they tell you about the type of place you feel drawn to?

You should now have a fleshed-out list of ideas underneath each of the three circles on your worksheet. It is fine if you wrote more under some circles than others. We would expect, however, that your larger circles will have produced more ideas than your smaller circles. If this is not the case, you might want to reconsider how you have sized your three circles.

STEP 3: Look for Common Themes

Now put on your detective hat. You are going to look at what you've written so far and try to find clues. These will come in the form of common themes—similarities between the various things you recorded in Step 2. Here are examples of the sorts of things people might discover about themselves as they do this:

> *"It seems like many of my answers revolve around how I tend to notice things that other people don't. Maybe I have a gift for keen observation."*

> *"I didn't realize that I gravitate to activities where I plan and*

structure other people's activities. I see that theme showing up over and over."

"What I notice is that I keep coming back to numbers. I guess I'm very quantitatively driven."

Grab some colored markers or pencils. Then read carefully through what you've written again, looking for common themes. When you spot them, highlight in a particular color all of the responses that relate to that theme. Feel free to draw arrows, connecting lines, or whatever else helps you make sense of what you are seeing.

STEP 4: Put the Picture Together

Now it's time to pull your circles together. This step is more like art than science. There isn't one right way to fit the pieces together. Rather, it's an interpretive exercise that encourages you to experiment and play with ideas.

As you work through this step, feel free to change the rules to fit your own ideas and instincts. If you feel your circles should morph into some other shape, or if you want to draw your map in some different way altogether, then do it. This is your exercise, after all.

For this step, you will first decide how your three circles relate to each other. Think about overlaps. Is your sense of passion (personal gifts and talents) directly related to a specific purpose (your cause)? If so, then those two circles should probably overlap a lot on your diagram. Find a large clean sheet of paper and begin sketching how you think your circles connect.

Below are a few examples of what your diagram might look like. To make things simpler, we will assume that the person drawing these diagrams has assigned equal importance to passion, purpose, and place, so all the circles are the same size. In your diagram, however, try to maintain the size differences of your circles as you draw your map.

CALLING

For the first example, let's say that you know your spiritual gifts and feel driven to use them (passion circle), that you feel drawn to a problem that needs your spiritual gifts (purpose circle), and that you are currently in a position (place circle) that allows you to use your gifts in service to your purpose. This, of course, is the epitome of calling—all three elements working together. If this scenario describes you, then your diagram might look something like this:

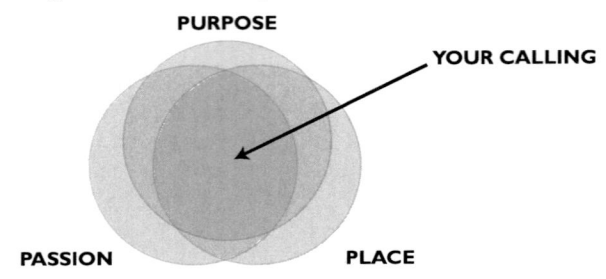

The overlap between these three circles creates a space in the middle that represents your personal sense of calling.

Drawing your map might also help you understand why you *haven't* yet found a sense of calling. Here are a few diagrams that depict misalignment between passion, purpose, and place:

Let's say that your workplace, wherever it is, makes good use of your gifts and talents. However, your work doesn't give you a sense of purpose. Perhaps you don't really believe in what the organization does. So, you have a healthy overlap between passion and place, but the purpose circle is disconnected, as follows:

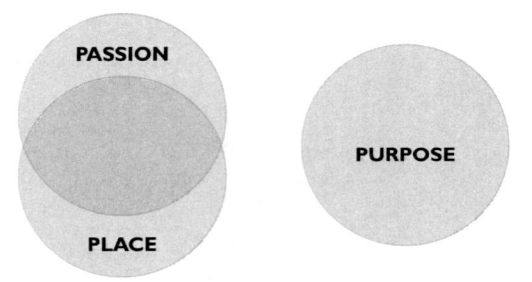

What if you work somewhere that promotes a cause you care about deeply, but you are required to do work that doesn't tap into your best gifts and talents? In that case, you would draw a strong overlap between purpose and place, but a disconnect with passion, as follows:

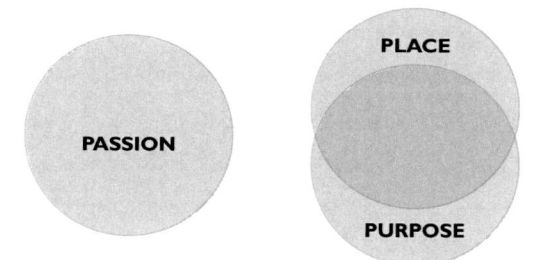

Another possibility is that you have a clear sense of your gifts and passions, and you know how they contribute to a purpose you care about, but you aren't in a role that allows you to use your passions in pursuit of your cause. You may be in the wrong job to pursue your calling, or perhaps you don't have a job at all. In either case, your diagram might look something like this:

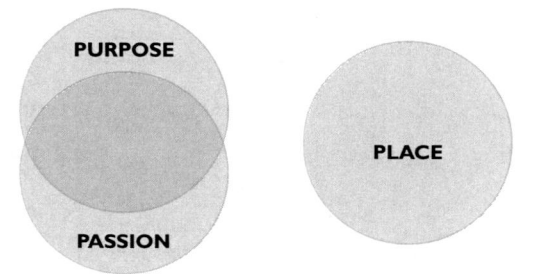

Lastly, perhaps none of your circles have come together yet. Maybe you don't know what your gifts are, or what cause you want to pursue. Or maybe, even if you do feel drawn to some passion, purpose, or place, you cannot see a way to get there. If any of these is the case, your diagram may simply be three non-overlapping circles. This is *not* cause for despair! It only means that you are still on your journey to identify your calling in life. The next two steps of the exercise may give you insights to help you bring your circles closer together. Once you have drawn your map, you can continue on to the next step.

STEP 5: Chart the Terrain

On any good map, the topography is well-labeled. For the fifth step, you will add written descriptors into your diagram to identify the terrain. As you do this, you might find that you want to go back and change the size or orientation of your original circles. That is perfectly fine.

First, consider the overlaps between the circles you drew in Step 4. How would you describe the space where they intersect? Start labeling those spaces in your diagram. For instance, one of our zookeeper friends might have a big overlap between passion and place. She might write the following in that space: "My zoo gives me lots of opportunities to interact with the public to educate them about primates, which is what I love to do most." Give some thought to all of the overlaps in your diagram.

If all three circles intersect somewhere in your diagram, pay special attention to that shared space among them. What you write in that intersection may help you capture the essence of your calling. For instance, a nurse might write in that section: "My calling is to use my spiritual gifts for compassion, communication, as well as my expertise in health care, to offer comfort and dignity for terminally ill patients in my current role as a palliative care nurse." (Notice how this statement incorporates all three calling components: a passion for compassionate care, the purpose of providing end-of-life comfort, and a place in the role of palliative care nurse that brings passion and purpose together.)

After you have done your best to label the overlaps in your diagram, consider how you would describe the areas that *don't* overlap. These represent opportunities for you to increase your sense of calling in the future. For instance, if your passion circle overlaps very little with the other circles, it probably means you have some important spiritual gifts that you aren't currently able to use. You might label that non-overlapping portion of your circle as follows: "I have always excelled at spatial

Mapping Out Your Life's Work: An Exercise

reasoning and love visual problems and puzzles. But I never get to use this skill to any worthwhile purpose." There may be hundreds of gifts you can think of that you don't use regularly, but try to hone in on the ones that are most important to you.

If your purpose circle has a large non-overlapping section, label it by describing the causes you wish you could champion in the future. For instance, someone might label this as: "I would like to help children learn to love reading, but I don't have opportunities to do that, and I'm not sure whether I'd be good at it."

If your place circle has a large non-overlapping section, label it by describing things that your current role or job require you to do, but which don't fit well with your sense of passion and purpose. For instance, someone might write, "My work requires me to spend lots of time interacting with clients, but I'm a numbers person and feel uncomfortable and out of place talking to people directly."

There are other ways you might wish to label your map. You might want to draw additional diagrams, lines, or arrows to help you make sense of your passions, purpose, and place. Be as creative as you like and tailor your map to your own ideas and feelings. You are the only audience that really matters.

To help you out, we have provided some examples in Appendix 2 that show people's labeled diagrams. Use these to generate ideas, not as templates.

One last idea: while doing the exercise, some of our students have realized that their calling maps might have looked very different in the past, and that diagramming their previous map would help them better understand where they are now. You might want to try diagramming what your calling map looked like at different stages in your life to help you understand the choices you have made and the reasons you are doing the work you do today.

STEP 6: Make a Travel Plan

Now that you have mapped out your best guess at your personal calling, it's a good time to consider the next phase of your life journey. Proceed prayerfully with this step, and counsel with other important people in your life. Before you proceed, spend some time thinking and talking about the following types of questions:

- What opportunities are there for me to use my passions more?
- What can I do to contribute more to purposes I care about?
- How can I influence the place I'm in (my current situation, role, or job) so that it takes better advantage of what I have to offer?
- What things are keeping me from finding a sense of calling? How can I change them?
- How has the hand of the Lord led me to where I am now? What am I learning about my passion and purpose from the doors that Heavenly Father has opened for me?
- Am I being patient, and allowing the Lord to gradually lead me to my calling in life? Am I doing my best to use my gifts even if I don't feel like I'm in the perfect place yet?

None of these questions is easy. Nor do they directly lead to a step-by-step plan. However, if you prayerfully consider what you learned as you worked through this book, the Lord will implant in your mind and heart new ideas about how you can better use your spiritual gifts to serve His children. As a final step of this exercise, we urge you to develop a personal "travel plan"—to identify at least one thing, if not more, that you will start to do *now* to pursue your calling in life.

Write down some commitments to yourself. Be as concrete as you can, and make specific plans to carry them out. What will you do next? When will you start? What resources do you need? Who do you need to consult with? Try to address all of these questions so that you have a very precise plan of action.

And then, follow it!

A Final Story

Once upon a time, a young college graduate named Gary dreamed of getting a PhD in chemistry and teaching at a university. But he also had to provide for his wife and baby son, so he accepted a high school teaching job instead. Several years later, when he investigated PhD programs again, he found that the market for science professors was completely saturated. He returned to his high school teaching, somewhat discouraged.

As his family grew, Gary decided to leave teaching. He took a job as a chemist for the state government. This job allowed him to work in a lab and paid a good wage, but he found it less than challenging. At a friend's urging, he took a gamble and left science to sell insurance. Almost immediately he was miserable. Selling insurance was a very poor fit for his gifts. In dire financial straits, he took a job managing a relative's electronics store. After a few years, it folded. Gary was now middle-aged, and felt adrift. Not only had he missed his PhD dream, he was in financial distress and unsure about what to do next.

Gary was also a man of great faith. Despite all the turmoil, he remained devoted to the Lord, and felt guided in many of the choices he had made. So, why had he struggled so much? Could he ever find stability and professional purpose?

Twelve years had passed since Gary left the classroom. After much prayer, fasting, and soul-searching with his wife, he decided to renew his teaching certificate and go back to teaching high school. He knew all too well that he wouldn't make much money, but he had fond memories of his students. He knew he had a gift for teaching young people.

CALLING

He was hired at a high school near his boyhood home—literally going back to where he had started.

The work wasn't easy. Gary sometimes fought political battles, dealt with unmotivated students, and put in heavy hours of preparation—all for little pay. But he also rediscovered the difference teachers make in their students' lives. He soon became one of the most popular teachers in the school. When he retired, some 20 years later, the outpouring from fellow staff, students, and the community was overwhelming. Many wondered how the high school could continue without him. He had left a legacy of excellence and service that had influenced countless lives.

Gary is Jeff's father. And Jeff was the baby boy for whom he first sacrificed his dream of getting a PhD. Jeff reflects:

> *My father's experience is one reason I care so deeply about the quest for a calling in life. My dad did find his calling. Or, rather, his calling found him. But the journey was rocky and bewildering. Twenty years ago, he might have considered his professional life a failure. But when I'm with my dad in his town, we frequently bump into his former students. They inevitably stop and thank him for helping them to find their path. I couldn't feel prouder.*

In the eternal scheme of things, job descriptions really don't matter much. All the anxiety you feel about what to do with your life, how to impress people, how to land a job, or how to get ahead, will seem trivial when the Lord's grand plan for your eternal destiny is fully revealed. It won't matter if you were a bus driver or a CEO, a manicurist or a television celebrity, a street sweeper or the President of the United States. Any of those titles will be as nothing compared to the title "heirs of God and joint-heirs with Christ" (Romans 8:17).

What *will* matter is whether you served your fellowmen like the Savior did. Work is a wonderful way to do that. But work isn't an end in itself. It is a means for you to practice discipleship, as is every other worthwhile activity in your life.

Jeff's father is no longer in the classroom. But he continues to use his spiritual gift for inspiring young people through Church service and missions. He also uses what he learned by managing a retail store in his administrative assignments at Church. He uses the skills he learned in his short-lived insurance career to help him speak persuasively to people. Indeed, every twist and turn of his circuitous career path has enabled him to serve in some particular way to build the Lord's kingdom.

The path to your calling will be utterly unique. It won't look like Jeff's or Stuart's or Gary's, or that of any other person we described in this book. But if you make it a spiritual journey, then your career path will be exactly what you need, and exactly what allows you to serve Heavenly Father in a way only *you* can.

You have a calling in life. You are in the middle of the journey. And if you use your God-given spiritual gifts as a guide, you can be completely confident that your calling will find you.

Endnotes

1. http://www.guardian.co.uk/lifeand

Notes

Notes

Notes

APPENDIX 1

Examples of Step 2

CALLING

Jeff's Example

PASSION | **PURPOSE** | **PLACE**

PASSION

I feel like I was born to teach (I did "make believe" teaching as a child)

I love standing in front of a crowd when I'm excited about what I'm sharing. (Experience of feeling "butterflies at the blackboard")

I'm a good writer, and I love polishing prose.

I have a flair for the dramatic. I can deliver a punch line. I use emotion to communicate.

I love connecting with people on a deep, personal, spiritual level.

I crave quiet time and solitude.

I am spellbound by history.

Nothing excites me more than live theatre.

People seek me out as a listener.

I enjoy solving word puzzles and brain teasers.

PURPOSE

I get very energized by helping young people prepare for a new important chapter in their lives (e.g., MTC job, teaching BYU students)

I want my work to contribute to building the Kingdom of God.

I have felt that it's my purpose to assist people in finding their calling in life. Giving my devotional felt like a defining moment in finding my purpose.

I seem to be most effective at helping people of faith so that I can point them to divine assistance.

I feel deeply moved by issues related to social justice and human respect.

PLACE

The first time I stepped onto BYU campus, I felt like I was meant to be there.

I can't imagine being happier anywhere than on a university campus.

I have found that I need to believe strongly in the organization I'm with in order to feel any motivation (e.g., dark days at my corporate job).

I crave being part of a team that shares my commitment. I'm a "band of brothers" kind of guy.

When I think about how I got where I am, it is absolutely clear to me that the hand of God led me (sometimes kicking and screaming)

There is no other place in the world I would rather be working than where I am right now. My department feels like a permanent home.

Examples of Step 2

Anna's Example

(Anna is a Chinese graduate student with a background in journalism)

PASSION — **PURPOSE** — **PLACE**

PASSION

All of my hobbies (movies, music, photography) seem to be related to documenting people's lives.

I love travelling and embracing different cultures.

I have a talent for learning languages. I am a good writer (in Chinese). I always got the highest score in English class when I was in China.

I love dealing with big data sets, technology, and social media.

I like to connect with people personally.

I need quiet time.

People often ask me for advice. I tend to give advice more on an emotional basis than a logical basis.

PURPOSE

I feel a strong sense of accomplishment when I work on a news report, as I get to tell a true story to others who didn't know it before.

I have felt that it's my purpose to help unfold something in a more creative and objective way to those who do not get a chance to know about it, like introducing China to Americans, and introducing the Church to mainland Chinese people.

I care a lot about cultural differences, humanities and economics.

I want to use technology and social media to share my voice.

PLACE

When I first came to the United States in 2011, I had a feeling that I was supposed to be here.

My most meaningful jobs were working as a Chinese tutor, as a research assistant in Chinese government, and interning with a travel agency serving Chinese tourists. I tend to feel very deeply connected to the place where I work.

I can see that God has guided my path to be in certain places.

I have a strong feeling I would be most effective working in a multi-cultural organization.

Wendy's Example

(Wendy is Director of Womens Basketball Operations at BYU and is deeply involved in a youth nonprofit)

PASSION

I enjoy connecting with youth.

I am passionate about sports and physical movement.

I have had a lot of experiences with helping young adults work toward their goals.

I am happiest when I am cleaning—my house, other people's houses. I love to help make things organized and orderly.

I love inspiring other people.

PURPOSE

I really want to help underprivileged kids achieve and strive for better things.

I feel compelled to teach.

I get really excited about helping kids to know their worth and to discover their abilities.

I am particularly drawn to people who are beating the odds—recovering addicts, people experiencing poverty and illiteracy, etc.

My purpose has to include basketball.

PLACE

I belong at a university.

I feel a deep connection to the Pacific Islands, and feel like I need to work with young Islanders.

I need to work at a place where my co-workers share my values.

APPENDIX 2

Examples of Step 4

CALLING

Jeff's Example

PASSION

I supplement my work life with involvement in theatre to express my desire to share stories that move people

PURPOSE

My job allows me to use my teaching gifts to prepare idealistic people of faith for public service. BYU feels like the perfect place for me to blend my faith with my intellectual pursuits.

My research allows me to contribute to BYU through my writing talents, but I notice that I don't feel a deep sense of purpose in some of my research obligations. I need to better align my research with purposes that matter to me.

PLACE

Some of my job's administrative demands take me away from my talents and passions, but I'm still glad I can contribute.

Notice in Jeff's example:

- Jeff's sense of "Purpose" is almost completely subsumed in "Place." Working at BYU almost entirely fulfills his sense of purpose

- He has a lot of passions (not all listed) that aren't addressed through his work, so he strives to get involved in many non-work activities.

- He realized that he needs to be more strategic in choosing research projects so that they align better with his sense of purpose.

Examples of Step 4

Anna's Example

I need to further develop my English writing and oral speaking skills in order to realize my passion.

PLACE

To prepare for my calling, I need to keep working at part-time jobs teaching Chinese and developing a stronger bridge between the US and China.

PASSION

My calling would allow me to use my linguistic and communication skills to share my thoughts about culture and religion through technology.

I have a strong sense of what I want to do, but I haven't yet mustered the motivation to plan my path carefully.

PURPOSE

Notice in Anna's example:

- Anna is very early in her career. This exercise helped her to see some steps she needs to take to bring her three circles in closer alignment.

CALLING

Wendy's Example

PURPOSE

I am not as directly involved as I would like to be in tackling the far-reaching problems of poverty and illiteracy.

My passion for cleaning things seems to apply to my purpose. Maybe my calling is to "clean people up and get them on their way." I want to combine my passion for inspiring youth with the purpose of helping the underprivileged (particularly Pacific Islanders). My job doesn't do that directly, but my nonprofit work does.

My passion for cleaning physical things doesn't really apply at my work.

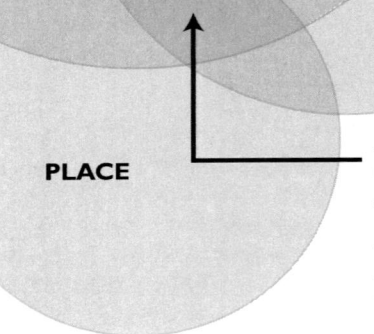

PASSION

PLACE

My job does allow me to inspire young people who are starting out in life. It doesn't give me direct access to the underprivileged, however.

Notice in Wendy's example:

- Wendy's three circles don't have a large overlap. Even though she loves her job, it doesn't give her opportunities to work on her sense of purpose.
- However, Wendy has supplemented her work with nonprofit involvement that almost perfectly combines her passion and purpose.
- The exercise helped Wendy discover that her passion for cleaning may have broader application: cleaning up people's lives. This was a meaningful insight for her.

Acknowledgments

We have been thinking about and studying professional callings for many years now. We can't begin to count or adequately acknowledge all of the people along the way who shaped our thinking, inspired us with their stories, corrected us when we were off the path, and encouraged us in our endeavors. We are the recipients of countless kindnesses and great ideas. We apologize in advance to those whose contributions we have overlooked in these acknowledgments.

First, we pay tribute to the generous folks who allowed us to invade their privacy and use their stories and quotes in this book. They include Leonard Anderson, Bob Chapman, Ladeena Christensen, David Gibbs, Michael Gates Gill, Ken Hansen, Sam Hymas, Dr. Dale Hull, Eli Jones, Nick LaRosa, Michelle Linford, Kathryn Little, Trevor Manning, Santiago Michalek, Jim Mortenson, Jacqueline Munns, Steve Searles, Matt Taylor, Noah Van Cott, Lucie Wehrmeister, and Matt Youngs. We also offer heartfelt thanks to a handful of friends who wished their stories and involvement in the book to remain entirely anonymous. We are grateful to Wendy Anae and Anna Gong for allowing us to use their excellent calling maps as examples.

We have also benefitted immeasurably from a small and incredibly supportive community of scholars who share our passion for studying meaningful work. Through countless conversations and playful explorations together, our ideas have become so enmeshed with theirs that it's impossible to tease apart who they "belong" to. So, we simply celebrate the collective learning community. Some of those whose ideas and encouragement have blessed our work include Professors Michel Anteby (Harvard University), Sue Ashford (University of Michigan), Marya Besharov (Cornell University), Jeff Bednar (Brigham Young University), John Bingham (Brigham Young University), Teresa Cardador (University of Illinois), Briana Caza (Griffith University), Katie DeCelles (University of Toronto), Shasa Dobrow (London School of Economics and Political Science), Jane Dutton (University of Michigan), Karen Golden-Biddle (Boston University), Adam Grant (Wharton School of Business), Spencer Harrison (Boston College), Glen Kreiner (Pennsylvania State University) Carrie Leana (University of Pittsburgh), Jacoba Lilius (Queen's University), David Mayer (University of Michigan), Andy Molinsky (Brandeis University), Michael Pratt (Boston College), Ryan Quinn (University of Louisville), Brent Rosso (Montana State University), Scott Sonenshein (Rice University), John Paul Stephens (Case Western Reserve University), Jennifer Tosti-Kharas (San Francisco State University), Heather Vough (McGill University), Monica Worline (University of California, Irvine), and Amy Wrzesniewski (Yale University), as well as Justin Berg (a doctoral student at Wharton School of Business), Kira Schabram, (a doctoral student at the University of British Columbia), and Kathryn Dekas (People Analytics Manager at Google).

We also owe a great debt of gratitude to friends and colleagues who provided insights about professional callings, who read early drafts of the book, or who gave us helpful advice and guidance as we prepared to publish it. Our thanks to Don Adolphson, Brad Agle, Bonnie Atkinson, Chris Banford, George & Carol Bauer, Catherine Cooper, Gary Cornia, Shailesh Deshpande, Sheri Dew, Margie Duffy, Rex Facer, Chris-

Acknowledgments

tine Hansen, David Hart, Stephanie Hibbert, Sherami Jara, Andrew Marshall, Kathleen McGinn, Aaron Miller, Peter Miller, Richie Norton, Alisa Hardy Orton, Joseph Ogden, Heather Pack, Tristi Pinkston, Josh Rohatinsky, Lisa Roper, Chris Schoebinger, Jeff Sessions, Gary & LaRaine Thompson, Joel Vallett, Larry Walters, Lori Wadsworth, and Eva Witesman. A special thanks to Kent Minson, of BYU Academic Publishing, for guiding us through the process of publishing this book.

Lastly, and most importantly, we thank the two most important people in our lives, Aimee Thompson and Maren Bunderson, for their constant cheerleading, personal sacrifices, inspiration and unconditional love.